DO YOU KNOW

Where to pan for gold in San Francisco?
Where to look for precious agates and jasper?
The best Bay Area museums for kids?
The most exciting playgrounds?
Places to picnic where you can sift the "middens" of ancient Indian civilizations?

THE GREAT FAMILY FUN GUIDE TO SAN FRANCISCO

is the first guidebook to offer a complete spectrum of standard and unusual activities, taking into consideration attention spans, limits of energy and proximity of attractions so that everyone will enjoy the trip.

THE
GREAT
FAMILY
FUN GUIDE
TO
SAN FRANCISCO!

Franz T. Hansell

BALLANTINE BOOKS • **NEW YORK**

For my son Franz
whose question, "What are we going to do today, Dad?"
started it all . . .

SBN 345-23976-8-195

First Printing: July 1974

Printed in the United States of America

Cover photo by Peter Fronk
Back cover and interior photos by James Barker

A Comstock Edition

BALLANTINE BOOKS
A Division of Random House, Inc.
201 East 50th Street, New York, N.Y. 10022
Simultaneously published by
Ballantine Books, Ltd., Toronto, Canada

Contents

Introduction

"San Francisco's a real grown-up town."—Frank Sinatra.

"Let's go to San Francisco!"

The whole family is excited at the prospect of a good vacation. San Francisco is a magic name. It's excitement, sophistication, and adventure. San Francisco means a *real* Chinatown, and the Gold Rush, and cable cars, views, Alcatraz, *Bullitt,* hippies, beatniks, sea lions, and the Golden Gate Bridge. It means earthquakes (the big quake of 1906 and the one that might strike right now while you're reading this), and ships along the Embarcadero and the bright lights along Broadway. San Francisco means a certain feeling in the air that has mixed in it the sailors who were shanghaied in the Barbary Coast days and the current season of grand opera, the Raiders and 49ers, the Giants and the Athletics. It's a wonderful town: people enjoy it immensely.

But just because San Francisco is called "America's favorite city" it doesn't mean automatic enjoyment for the visitors touring with children. Many of the most advertised highlights of San Francisco are adult in nature and lost on kids. Our magnificent views (indeed, any view—unless they can climb on it) have

1

little meaning to the seven-and-under crowd. San Francisco's famed night life and world-renowned restaurants delight adults, but are out of reach for children—except for teen-agers, and sometimes even for them. Chinatown, to the unprepared, can be an endless nightmare of schlock shops where the ten-and-under will "gimme" you to death. The same is true of our elegant shops. These shops are some of the best in the Western Hemisphere, but they bore children. Many visits have been spoiled because the touring parents didn't know what to do with the kids in San Francisco.

What to do with the kids is also a week-to-week problem with families who live in the Bay Area. That might sound farfetched, but not so at all. Where to go is a matter of word of mouth, discovery, research, and luck. I was born and raised in Springfield, Ohio, and thought I knew the region like the back of my hand. On a recent visit, imagine my astonishment when my brother-in-law took me to a working grist mill only eight miles from town that had been in continuous operation since 1805! My parents had never taken me there; I'd never heard of it from neighbors; in the three summers I worked at the Boy Scout camp, four miles away, I got not a whiff of the place. If that can happen in a small place like Springfield, Ohio, imagine the undiscovered treasures missed by Bay Area families.

There is no reason for the Bay Area family ever to be bored or for the touring family not to have a glorious vacation here. I know of no other single region so rich with activities for children, natural, historic, and cultural. It's the easiest place to balance a visit for the enjoyment of the whole family—the toddlers, preschoolers, kids (six to eleven), preteen-agers, teenagers, and, of course, parents. That spectrum is a huge diversity of interests, spans of concentration, limits of boredom and energy—all of which must be accommodated. The book is directed primarily to the tourist traveling with his family and always offers the easiest and most important attractions first. The tourist wants to see the highlights and has the added difficulty of feeding and housing his flock in a strange place—always a complicated and time-consuming endeavor. The touring family must keep loose, as anyone who has traveled with kids knows. Changes in itinerary are an hour-to-hour, sometimes minute-to-minute, thing. For this reason, the book will offer much more information than the tourist could ever cram into his schedule, no matter what his time allowance. These alternatives will prevent the touring family from being stuck with time to kill—there's another attraction fifteen minutes away. But what are alternatives for the tourist are good things for the Bay Area family to plan to do.

The book covers an area roughly fifty miles in radius from San Francisco—from Russian River to the north to San Jose–Santa Cruz to the south.

Included here are two handy features that should be included in every guidebook, though I've seen them in none of the available books. The first is hints on what to do with the kids when the adults want to tour adult things. San Francisco shops are unique and should not be missed by anyone visiting here. Shopping with children, though, is a deadly undertaking. Fortunately, in San Francisco anyway, the most delightful shopping areas are close to attractions that are fascinating to kids. In each case, I'll show where one parent can take the kids while the other shops: it's a toss-up as to who will get the most enjoyment out of his adventure.

The second feature is a list of good shops for kids. One of the amenities of a big city is the availability of hard-to-get things—you have to send away for them back home. Here you'll find a list of San Francisco and Bay Area toy stores and shops that cater to hobbyists—where to get replacements for chemistry sets; telescope mirror blanks; sheet music; model train-car-boat-plane supplies; coin, stamp, and lapidary outlets; as well as leather, mosaic, art, handicraft, stained glass, jewelry, and basketry stuff—where to get good paper for kites, netting needles for making your own crab net, knitting needles and wool, electronic parts (new and surplus), camping and backpacking gear. I've also included a few shops that sell supplies seldom seen anywhere (ship's chandlery for example) just because they are neat shops for kids and adults. If your preteen-ager or teen-ager is interested in a foreign culture, the book includes the shops that sell the crafts and food of foreign lands (where to buy poi, frozen banana leaves, Arabic bread, Spanish, Greek, German, Russian books and records) and a sampling of foreign restaurants.

In all cases, the directions will be from Union Square in San Francisco (the most central spot downtown). Those attractions outside the city will include the traveling time if they are more than an hour away. The boredom factor varies from little kid to little kid and you might want to choose something else to see if you know you'll be stuck too long in the car with a fretful child.

The book starts with the good places in San Francisco to take kids (all the major attractions are listed, the more adult being merely noted), then goes south, north, and east. Parts of the book overlap because, so often here, the natural attraction blends with the sporting and cultural aspects of a place. Beautiful Coyote Park in Fremont, for example, offers wild country to walk through, Indian mounds being excavated by University of California archaeologists and the Bio-Sonar Laboratories that study large sea mammals. Fleishhacker Zoo in San Francisco is near Lake Merced, where one may fish for trout, and Ocean Beach, where one may fish for striped bass and find gold-bearing sands and fossil-bearing rocks on the beach—all within walking distance of each other (two to three miles).

Yes, there's gold to be found within San Francisco, and semiprecious stones, but, more, there are grand experiences to be had at every turn. There's no better place for the family to vacation than San Francisco and the Bay Area. The calendar of events will give you the dates of everything of special interest to kids from the county-fair dates to when the shad are running in Russian River; from when the Giants are playing to when the whales are migrating; from the general dates when you can watch the Ringling Brothers Circus to the best time to see an egret hatching or watch the blessing of the fishing fleet. And with that for a countdown, we're off!

1

San Francisco: An Explanation Before You Start

SAN FRANCISCO is a curious place geographically, historically, and culturally. On the southern peninsula of the only natural opening of the Coast Range for fifty miles on either side—the opening is the Golden Gate—San Francisco has upside-down weather. The cold Japanese Current is about 55 degrees, summer and winter. In the summer, the great interior valley of California becomes extremely hot: temperatures ranging from 95 to 106 degrees are common. Vegetables of all kinds grow like crazy (the Sacramento–San Joaquin Valley is one of the most productive spots on earth), but the hot interior sucks cold air through the Golden Gate from the sea, across San Francisco, so our summer months are the most miserable of the year—cold, foggy, and damp. San Francisco is one of the few places in the world where you may experience a fifty-degree temperature drop by traveling *down* toward sea level. In Sacramento it might be 105 degrees—hot and muggy, and you're sweating to death. An hour later and you're in San Francisco, and your ears are hurting from the 55-degree cold, windy fog. If you come in the summer months, bring sweaters and be prepared for the cold. Actually, you have to wear things you can peel off. The mornings and

7

evenings are cold; the middle of the afternoon is warm. It works both ways, of course. Spring and autumn are our hottest months, and, during the winter, the temperature seldom drops below 55 degrees. Flowers bloom and grass must be cut all year around here—when the surrounding countryside is indeed cold.

Historically and culturally, San Francisco is also curious. Looking at the solid public buildings, hearing its name mentioned in the same breath with other world cities, might make one assume that San Francisco is an old city. Not so at all. San Francisco Bay, one of the largest landlocked natural harbors in the world, wasn't even discovered by Europeans until 1769. The summer fogs that cool the city hid the Golden Gate inlet so effectively that all the great explorers-adventurers-pirates of history missed it. Sir Francis Drake passed the Bay in the 1500's and landed up the coast at what is now Point Reyes National Seashore to scrape his boats. The Bay, which at that time was seven hundred square miles of water, was stumbled upon by a party on horseback looking for *Monterey Bay!* The sites for the Presidio and the Mission were laid out in 1776 and San Francisco dates its beginning from then. Now, 1776 is a fairly old date for an American city, but San Francisco wasn't a city then. It wasn't even a town seventy years later, when Charles Dana was here in 1836. It was barely a village.

San Francisco for all intents and purposes did not exist until the discovery of gold in 1848. Then it became an instant city—no, an instant metropolis. This great city is only a little more than a hundred years old. Physically, it's even younger than that. The earthquake-fire of 1906 leveled nine-tenths of the city. In the whole downtown area from Van Ness Avenue to the Bay, there are few pre-earthquake buildings standing. It was not the earthquake that devastated the area, although many buildings were knocked down or severely damaged. It was the fire that followed that did the worst work. The earthquake ruptured the water mains and water service pipes. Pressure failed in the mains and the firemen were without means of fighting fire. The myriad little fires (remember, this was the age of wood or coal cook stoves and gas lighting) raged out of control, joined together, and became a fire storm. The fire was capricious, leveling whole areas and sparing a few structures. The decorator shops along Jackson and Pacific Streets were part of the old Barbary Coast, and they survived; the homes of the rich on Nob Hill didn't. It was from this, and from the subsequent messages from the pulpit that San Francisco's wickedness had caused it all, that Charles Field wrote the gleeful poem:

> If, as they say, God spanked the town,
> For being over frisky,
> Why did He burn his Churches down,
> And spare Hotaling's Whiskey?

The round brick circles you see in the intersections of the city are safeguards against future water failure. They outline huge permanent cisterns (there is a manhole in the center so you can identify them) which the fire department can use if the water mains are broken again.

The Gold Rush brought young men from all over the world to try their luck in the gold fields. From the beginning, San Francisco had a huge mixture of nationalities: North and South Americans, Europeans, and people from the South Seas and the Orient. It wasn't a wholly joyous intermixing. Racial and ethnic prejudice, then as now, was rampant. The Chinese were especially put upon. The workers were brought in by the shiploads to provide cheap labor in the mines and on the railroads. They were feared because there were so many of them and because they worked so hard and lived on so little. Foreign workers in the gold fields were heavily taxed (that is, non-English-speaking foreigners), and nationality groups formed their own neighborhoods in San Francisco, as in every other big city in America (and abroad).

The thing that makes San Francisco different is that all those who came here were out for the main chance and those who made it were respected, no matter their origin. William Leidesdorff, a pioneer black businessman and vice-consul under Mexican rule, has a street named for him in the heart of the financial district and is buried in the Mission Dolores. The Irish, who were universally disrespected in the 1840s and 1850s, fought their way to the top of the municipal government, and the put-upon Chinese turned the idea of ghetto upside down in San Francisco. Ghetto implies a shutting out, a confinement of peoples of a different race or religion. The Chinese were yellow, heathen, and foreign. The Chinese were also followers of super-American ethics—reverence for older people, care and education of the children, frugality, hard work, civic duty (their own welfare system), sharp trading, and loyalty to their traditions. But instead of being "shut out" of San Francisco, they shut San Francisco out to guard their way of life. Even today, Chinatown is proudly American, but also proudly Chinese.

The great numbers of different nationality groups in the city permit the visitor to sample the best points of each without going abroad. The best part of our nationality districts is that they aren't fake, contrived, quaint places. They are real working neighborhoods. We'll look at them later.

Of the major American cities, San Francisco is unique in that it is growing more attractive to the visitor every year. It's one city that's not dying but developing. In the last ten years, wonderful things have appeared: Ghirardelli Square, the Cannery, the Historic Ships State Park, the Old Mint, Fort Point

National Monument, the Exploratorium, Vaillancourt Fountain. Hotels are being built at a crazy pace and at the moment (and probably for several years hence), San Francisco has an overabundance of hotel rooms. This means a break for the tourist. Before you get a motel room, call the major hotels. There are real bargains to be had. A half-hour stop at the Visitors and Convention Bureau for a list might get you accommodations that you didn't expect for the money.

One final point: don't worry about getting very lost in San Francisco. It's a small city, physically, only about seven miles to a side. There are only four major roads into and out of it: Highway 101 across the Golden Gate Bridge to the north; Highway 80 across the Bay Bridge east to Oakland; Highway 101 going south along the edge of the Bay, and Highways 1 or 280 down the middle of the peninsula or along the ocean. In town, the streets are largely gridded like a waffle iron, bisected by Market Street, which goes from the Ferry Building to Twin Peaks. Every service station, hotel, and motel comes equipped with a city map. You shouldn't have any trouble.

It's impossible, of course, to list current attractions in a general guide, or to state the price of something months in advance. Fortunately for the tourist, prices of restaurants, etcetera, are provided by the Visitors Bureau in a weekly list of events—available in every hotel and motel lobby. The pink section of the Sunday *Examiner-Chronicle* carries a complete listing of current movies, lectures, plays, musical events, museums, and local and regional events—as well as who's appearing in the local nightclubs, etcetera. Both the map and the current-events guide are extremely valuable. There is a new weekly magazine at this writing, named *City*, that is also handy. With the help of these aids and this book, you should have a glorious visit in San Francisco and the Bay Area.

2

Cable Cars and Fisherman's Wharf

IN A CITY as full of attractions as San Francisco, there is always a problem of what to do first (after you get your family in a hotel or motel). Touring is exhausting and driving to get somewhere in a car creates a certain inertia that makes you just want to keep sitting. The only thing to do is to get out at once and into the city. The cable cars are the best way to make the plunge.

Cable Cars

There is no more exhilarating public transportation in the world than the San Francisco cable car. In constant use since 1873 as the most efficient way to get over San Francisco's hills, the cable cars are still heavily used by both tourists and residents. They are a regular part of the Municipal Railroad System, and transfers to or from the bus and streetcar lines are available.

Their operation is simplicity itself. Beneath the streets where the cable cars run is an endless wire rope—the cable. All the cables in the city are powered by the huge engines and wheels in the Cable Car Barn at Washington and Mason Streets (see page 105). The cables travel at a constant speed. To make the cars go, the gripman pulls the handle that clamps the car onto the cable and away you go on a rattling, bumpy ride straight up into the clouds, it seems— not unlike a roller coaster. You are positive that you won't make it up the hills and begin to pray when you come down. Be sure to listen to the signal bells. Everybody holds on dear life and enjoys it immensely. Ringing the cable car's bells is such an art that there is a contest in the spring for the best bellringer of all.

Each of these cars is made by hand. When a new one is needed, all the usable parts of a car no longer in service are stripped and incorporated into the "new" one. The other pieces are made by skilled carpenters, cabinetmakers, blacksmiths, and machinists, all by hand. The brakes or undercarriage might be new, but the seat you're sitting on might be the same one President Theodore Roosevelt sat on when he was here to dedicate the Dewey Memorial in 1900; or Enrico Caruso, when he gave a concert here in 1906.

There are three cable lines still running. Two of them, the Hyde Street and the Powell Street lines, start at Market Street and Powell and end in the Fisherman's Wharf area. The third line runs along California Street from Market, up over Nob Hill, to Van Ness Avenue.

The HYDE STREET LINE is the best ride. It will take you up Nob Hill (a block from the top are the Mark Hopkins and Fairmont Hotels); thence to Russian Hill, where you'll enjoy a sweeping view of the Bay; a glimpse down Lombard Street (the crookedest street); then you'll hold on for dear life down Hyde Street hill—scary but safe. It ends at Victorian Park near Ghirardelli Square, Aquatic Park, the Cannery, Historic Ships Museum, and the west side of Fisherman's Wharf.

The POWELL STREET LINE also crosses the slopes of Nob Hill, skirts Chinatown and North Beach, and ends at Taylor and Bay Streets, close to Cost Plus and

Akron (two famous discount import houses), the Cannery, Fisherman's Wharf, the *Balclutha,* Bay Cruises, the ferryboat to Tiburon, Angel Island, and Alcatraz, and helicopter rides over the Bay.

Board either of them anywhere on Powell Street from Market to California. It's fun to ride one out and the other back—their terminals are about six blocks from each other. In either case, you'll end up at FISHERMAN'S WHARF.

Fisherman's Wharf

San Francisco's Fisherman's Wharf is still a working fish-catching and processing center. There are real fishermen here, mostly crab fishermen. You're not likely to see them, though, because they keep fisherman's hours. They're usually out beyond the Golden Gate by 3 AM and have cleaned out their pots, unloaded their catch, and eaten their breakfast-supper by seven in the morning. The boats are there, though, and there's nothing more delicious than eating a freshly steamed crab caught only a few hours before.

We'll start at the end of the Hyde Street cable-car line. Most interesting to adults are the two vast shopping complexes that join each other at Hyde and Beach. Both are unique and both have facilities for entertaining little children, so the adults can look through the shops.

GHIRARDELLI SQUARE is a complex of buildings that contain fine shops and restaurants of every description. It used to be the old Ghirardelli (pronounced "Gear-ar-delli") chocolate and spice factory. Older kids like it because they can later say back home that they saw a dress that cost eight hundred dollars. Little kids, toddlers to five-year-olds, can be safely left at a glue-in. Here, for a modest price (50¢ at this writing), they are given an unlimited supply of oddly shaped pieces of wood and all the glue they can use to make —things. The middle kids, six to ten, might become a little antsy after a while, but, as you'll see, there are places to take them nearby if one parent wants to shop in earnest.

THE CANNERY, diagonally across the street, was just that. It was the old Del Monte fruit-canning factory. Again, this is a complex of buildings on several levels transformed into many shops and restaurants. In the Cannery is a ground-level patio with a snack bar (reasonable) that has outside tables where one may eat and watch a continuous performance of street musicians, mimes, and the like. These are real live people performing in public—not like on TV. The street musicians are a new and delightful addition to San Francisco. You'll find them on street corners, especially downtown, and at such places as Fisherman's Wharf and Union Street. By and large, they're good; some are very good. Outside TV, there are few places left where a competent musician or entertainer can make a living at his profession. There are very few restaurants that have live musicians, no variety shows or music halls where they can perform. Television has only so many channels. But they want to play, and the public wants to hear them, so they took to the streets and make a living from the quarters, half-dollars, and dollars you throw in their violin cases.

SAN FRANCISCO MARITIME MUSEUM. Corner of Polk and Beach Streets. Daily, 10 AM–5 PM. Free.

This is a good place to start. Just down the street from the cable-car terminal, the museum is a grand repository of ships models and anchors, figureheads and pieces of deepwater gear. Looking at the models and actual equipment will help to appreciate your visit to the historic ship and the *Balclutha* which we will cover later. There are a snack bar and rest rooms under the museum that open onto Aquatic Park.

AQUATIC PARK is one of the most fascinating public parks in San Francisco, mainly because it offers so many different new things to see. At the upper end of the park are sunbathers and the *bocce* courts. The stadium usually has three or four groups of musicians playing together for the fun of it. The Santana group started here. At the foot are a sandy beach and the Municipal Pier. We'll take them one by one.

The *bocce* courts are hard-packed sand alleys separated by boards. *Bocce* is the ancestor of bowling and closely related to bowling on the green. In the lanes, about the length of a bowling alley, a small ball is thrown to the end and the contestants try to bowl the larger balls (about the size of duck pin balls) close to it. It's something like shuffleboard in that opponents try to maneuver each other's balls out of good positions. It's an exciting sport, but one usually seen only in cities with large Italian populations.

The sandy beach is a good place to watch another seldom-seen sport—long-distance swimming. Put your toe in the water and you'll see why this is such an unusual sport. The water is cold enough to turn the ordinary mortal into a solid block of ice (the temperature runs about 55 degrees). One of the curiosities about San Francisco is that, though it is semicircled by ocean and bay, water everywhere, there are few places to go swimming in ocean or on the bay; this is especially so for small children or inexperienced swimmers. Unlike Aquatic Park, Ocean Beach is one of the best surfing beaches in the state, but the water is so cold that wet suits are required. Tides and currents are treacherous, so most beaches are posted against swimming and no life guards are on duty. Splashing along the edges of the ocean or Bay beaches is safe, but be careful. When my boy was a toddler, we were walking ankle deep along Ocean Beach. I stopped to look at the sand cliffs and the next moment, he was pulled off his feet and was headed for Hawaii. When he was six, and a strong, husky six, we were looking for sand dollars. He was caught around his knees by a surge of surf and bowled sideways for ten yards, in a sideways somersault. He couldn't get to his feet and might have been in trouble if I hadn't been there to help him. The Pacific Ocean and the Bay beaches, unless otherwise indicated, are to be treated with respect. In both incidents he had a wonderful time—in both incidents, I had bad dreams for weeks afterward.

The protected beach at Aquatic Park is safe enough for kids to splash around in, but swimming is still an ordeal. Of course, the temperature of the water and the vicious tides mean nothing to the long-distance swimmers. These hardy souls are out ploughing through the waves every day of the year—rain, sun, or freezing to death. Despite what you may have heard, it is possible to swim to Alcatraz. A stalwart women's swimming team once made it, and were one-upped by a men's team who swam to shore—handcuffed together! All the same, it's not a higly recommended activity in this book.

The MUNICIPAL PIER is one of the delights of the city for visitors and residents alike. It is at the end of Van Ness Street, at the northern end of Aquatic Park. On the way down the street from the *bocce* courts to the Pier, the buildings just beyond the snack bar are the San Francisco Sea Scouts headquarters. Someone is always there on weekends and usually on weekdays during the summer vacation. Visiting sea scouts and scoutmasters from other parts of the country might want to drop in and look at their facilities.

The municipal pier is a free pier. No fishing license is needed; there is no limit on catch or size. The pier is heavily used nearly every day of the year and the things you see there are fascinating. There is a constant movement up and down the half-mile of curving pier. You're walking a fair distance out into the exposed Bay, so the wind is always brisk, sometimes biting—a sweater is recommended even in summertime (you can get a sunburn and a cold at the same time), and the water-level view of the Bay, the city, and the ships coming through the Golden Gate is found nowhere else. The pier is heavily used, primarily because people catch a lot of fish there, and sharks and crabs and starfish. This is most interesting to people who have never seen salt-water fish alive. Fresh-water fishermen who have seen only bass and crappie, catfish, sunfish, and trout, are amazed and sometimes repelled by the appearance of some salt-water fish they've eaten as frozen fillets. Flounders and sole are definitely freaky with their sideways body and two eyes on one side of their heads. Ling cod and bullheads look like evil sea monsters (thank God they're small). And this is an interesting place to discover the eating habits of other nationalities. You'll see peoples of the Orient and Central and South American countries, whose borders are the ocean and whose diet and national cooking runs heavily to seafood, delight over the catch of a lot of little fish the whole of which would be rejected as non-keepers and unsuitable for an American fish fry. Ask them, as I did, what they do with little fish and it will open your eyes to new possibilties for your catches of little fresh-water fish. The West Coast South Americans, Peruvians and Chileans, incorporate them into rich fish stews. Now, fish stew or soup, to most Americans, sounds almost as attractive as a lard sandwich, but if you taste it at a Peruvian or Central American restaurant, you'll be amazed and delighted: six or seven kinds of fish cooked with vegetables in a spicy broth is a rich dish—tasting of fish, but not "fishy." The Philippinos take those little fish and grind them up into a purée, something like the

Italian anchovy paste, and use it for flavoring. You'll see people of many nationalities very happy to land a shark. Sharks are in the same family as swordfish; the first time I tasted shark steak, I couldn't tell the difference. I understand that some unscrupulous fish markets substitute it regularly, so it's likely you've eaten shark too.

Crabs are caught here too, and you'll see all the different kinds of crab traps and nets (we'll talk more about them in the fishing section of the Nature chapter). And the catching is the most exciting thing about Municipal Pier. You walk down it in a zig-zag course, looking at what the people are bringing in or have brought in. You can see the darndest things. As I related in the Comstock *An Opinionated Guide to San Francisco*, on one afternoon, I saw this guy looking foolish, with a bloody handkerchief wrapped around his fingers. A two-foot sand shark was twitching at his feet. "What happened?" I asked, and he said, "The hook was caught and I reached in his mouth to get it out, and he bit me!" The moral is, of course, don't put your fingers in sharks' mouths even if they're not man-eaters. The second thing was both pathetic and funny. There are a thousand sea gulls around Municipal Pier and they are great thieves. Put down a package of frozen anchovy bait and turn your back and one will bang down on it and be off. Most bait is usually soft and some will fly off the hook as you are casting, so the gulls chase it. Once I saw a sea gull catch the bait in mid air and swallow it, bait and hook. The man had a flapping, excited sea gull on the end of his line and didn't know what to do with it. He reeled it in like a living kite till it was ten feet from the end of his pole. A neighbor fisherman cut the line and the sea gull flew off in the direction of Alcatraz, squawking and bleeding at the beak. The man was sorry that he had hurt the bird and the other fishermen comforted him with shaggy-sea-gull stories—what they'd seen sea gulls eat and survive, what they'd seen sea gulls suffer and survive—how tough the sea gulls are. The people who fish on Municipal Pier are like that, and the things to be seen are rich, interesting, and unusual. Don't be afraid to talk with the fishermen. It's one of the few places anywhere you're able to go up to a perfect stranger of a different race, culture, or nationality and begin a conversation out of the blue with only, "Have you caught anything? What are you fishing for? What are you going to do with it?" And you'll get an answer. If you're timid, let your kids ask for you.

Directly down the hill from the Hyde Street cablecar terminus is one of the most unusual museums in this town of unusual museums—the four ships that comprise the SAN FRANCISCO MARITIME STATE HISTORIC PARK. Daily 10 AM–8 PM summer; 10 AM–6 PM winter. Admission: adults, 75¢; under 6 free.

The *Eureka* is the last paddle-wheel walking-beam ferry to operate on San Francisco Bay. It's an autopassenger ferry of the kind that was common before the two Bay bridges. Ferryboats are the most delightful way to get from here to there I can think of. One of the drawbacks to the ferryboat fleet was the traffic. All the boats entering and leaving San Francisco used the Ferry Building at the foot of Market Street. San Francisco is a peninsula, and the only way to get north or east was through the Ferry Building. The cars would be backed up for blocks on Market Street, especially on weekends and holidays. The bridges were a necessity, but they created their own problems —parking and congestion, smog and auto accidents. Ferries are coming back to San Fransico Bay. There are two lines now running (which we will see later) and a new fleet is to begin operation in 1975.

The good ferry *Eureka*, though, is an antique, as are the other three ships in this museum. The restoration of the ships is an ongoing process, which is being done with a good deal of imagination. The auto deck on the *Eureka* (just one side so far), is loaded with antique cars and trucks—Model Ts, Packards, Nashes, Dodges, and a Graham Paige, among others. The old newsstand upstairs is stocked with old periodicals and newspapers. There are viewing ports down into the engine room to let you see how a walking-beam paddle-wheeler operated (on the outside is a working model of the apparatus). With the admission price comes a set of earphones that receives beamed descriptions of what you're seeing at any point. Take them, but don't expect too much. They work as well as the earphones at the Smithsonian Institution in Washington, but those don't work very well either. The National Geographic Society in Washington and the Lawrence Hall of Science in Berkeley have a better system with pull-out earphones at each point of interest. There's no fading in and out with that system. In the Pilot's bridge at the top of the *Eureka*, the kids can steer the ship, at her moorings, with the huge wheel, and you get a glorious view of the Bay.

The *C. A. Thayer* is a three-masted coastal schooner. This and the little hay scow *Alma* were the workhorses of the Pacific coastal freight fleet. The *Thayer* was originally a lumber hauler, then went into the salt-fisheries business. In the hold, you can see the tiny space in which the fishermen-crew were packed —like sardines. Working on a ship was difficult and dangerous in the days of sail. The complicated rigging of the ship is a great place against which to photograph your kids. Grab hold of a piece of the ropes holding up the masts. They move and sing under your hand even though the ship is tied up to the dock. It will show you why canvas seamen spoke of ships as living things. The most impressive thing about these ships is that they aren't set pieces exhibited in glass cases. In no other museums in town, except the *Balclutha* and the Pioneer Fire Museum, do the kids get a taste of what it was really like in the "olden days."

The *Wapama* is a steam schooner built in 1915 that carried cargo (mostly lumber) and passengers between California ports and the Pacific Northwest. Most of the *Wapama*'s cargo was deck-stacked and piled high. We think of ships as mostly clean on top; the prints of old ships don't show the stowage of ten-foot and higher bulks of commodities on deck. Look at the new container ships sailing in and out of the Bay with boxed cargo stacked so high on deck that the ships look top-heavy and you'll get an idea of what the *Wapama*'s trim was when she was working.

The most fascinating part of this ship is the passenger section. It was cramped but gracious, something like a Pullman car. In this little ship is a tiny salon where they say people danced, a dining room for the passengers, a mess for the crew, and a smoking room for the gentlemen that was in fact a den for loafers and poker players. The passengers' cabins have been outfitted in the style of the period, and when you look through the portholes, you'll see antique toiletries sets or an old wireless radio receiver. The restoration of the *Wapama* is a continuing thing and every visit means another look at the facts of traveling by coastal steamer around the turn of the century. Steamships such as the *Wapama* were the only way to go from one of the big California coastal ports to the many little port cities from San Francisco north. They went out of business with paved roads and motorcars.

The *Alma* cannot be visited but only looked at—it's too low in the water. There were once about three hundred of these shallow-draft sailing "hay scows" that carried goods from San Francisco to the myriad little farms on the estuaries of San Francisco Bay and the Delta—and up the Sacramento and San Joaquin Rivers—and brought down produce, green goods, and hay from the farms to supply the dray horses in San Francisco before the motorcar and truck. The owner-sailors of these hay scows were as pugnacious as their landlubbing counterparts, the teamsters. What you're seeing in the *Alma* is a part of American transportation that got shunted aside, not because it didn't work, but because it didn't work as well as the other things that came along. The *Alma* hauled as much tonnage as the average truck, but it took them a day and a half to get to Sacramento with a load of cargo. A truck can do it in two hours.

Fisherman's Wharf Area

From the San Francisco Maritime State Historic Park, return up Hyde Street to the cable-car terminal, or turn left and head into the heart of Fisherman's Wharf itself. From Hyde and Jefferson Streets, walk toward the restaurants of Fisherman's Wharf to Taylor Street, then turn right and walk three blocks to Bay Street.

Let's begin at Market and Powell Streets and take the Powell Street cable car which will deliver you to a different set of attractions on Fisherman's Wharf. Board the Powell Street car, anywhere along Powell from Market Street up to Nob Hill and continue along Mason and the fringes of Chinatown and North Beach. For a nice walk down into Chinatown, through the residential fringes into the commercial heart of Chinatown at Grant, get off at Clay Street and walk down the three blocks to Grant Avenue. When you cross Stockton, look into the two alleys to your left. Spofford Alley and Waverly Place are almost like movie sets. If you get off the Powell Street cable car at Union Street and walk down to Columbus, you'll find yourself in the heart of the Italian shopping district of North Beach. Older kids and adults find this glimpse of yet another culture (signs in Italian, for example) very interesting. We'll come back to it later. The Powell Street car continues to the edge of Fisherman's Wharf.

The line ends at Bay and Taylor Streets, a rather curious place. On either side of you are the neat concrete buildings of a public housing project put up in the early 1950s. Down to the right a few blocks is the North Point complex, a private apartment development of expensive apartments indeed. This conjunction of Public Housing for the poor and private housing for the better-off doesn't seem to work in many other cities, but here it's working very well and has worked for a long time.

There are two great shopping centers near the end of the Powell Street line that are especially interesting to families traveling with children.

Straight ahead on Taylor Street is COST PLUS IMPORTS, a San Francisco landmark. It was the first large import discount house in the city. It dealt, and deals, in imported handicrafts. You'll find Mexican pottery and glassware, Philippine rattan and woodcarving, Spanish furniture, Near Eastern brassware, Indian mother-of-pearl inlay, a world of things that cost only a little more than if you buy them at far-flung native bazaars and ship them home yourself. None of what you see is absolutely essential, but all is nice to own. Cost Plus was a small place at first and became so firmly entrenched in San Francisco that it was common for the young people starting out to say that their apartment was furnished in Cost Plus and Salvation Army. The formula of "good goods" sold cheap has enabled the place to grow from one corner of a warehouse to three buildings. The quality of the stuff has increased (and so have the prices), but this is really a place where your allowance goes a long way in getting something out of the ordinary to take back home to Grandma and Grandpa. The three stores now in operation offer everything from handicrafts to antiques to a garden shop.

The NORTH POINT SHOPPING CENTER and AKRON are to your right down Bay Street when you get off the cable car. Both are in a rather small, two-story building, but there's a lot crammed into it. Akron, on the second floor, is a chain import (and domestic) discount house that runs more heavily to small appliances, household articles, and "useful" things than does Cost Plus. It also has great buys in clothing, hardware, kitchen wares, and art and garden supplies. Sometimes, you'll find imported bargains in their delicatessen as well as occasional wild buys. I bought a school-surplus desk with lifting desk top in excellent condition (seat attached) for $3.99. The Akron shop is on the upper level. On the lower level are an all-night supermarket; a drugstore; several boutiques; barber shops; a candy store that sells homemade goodies by the pound, so you can order a dab of this and a dab of that to satisfy the whole family; a bakery; an ice-cream parlor; a fish-and-chips stand; a coffee-and-doughnut stand; a hamburger and exotic wurst café, and, near the supermarket, a delicatessen that offers all kinds of cold salads, hot prepared foods (of the barbecued ribs, chicken, turkey, pork-fried-rice, and spaghetti- and meat-ball sort). It's a good idea to stop here to feed your kids before you venture into the higher prices of Fisherman's Wharf.

Fisherman's Wharf is developing into a very nice tourist attraction. As mentioned before, there are real fishermen working out of this area, and many seafood handlers and processors you never see work in the bleak warehouselike buildings on the short streets leading out over the water. These look like private, keep-out streets, but they are open to the public and it's interesting to poke around out there. Jefferson Street, the main street of Fisherman's Wharf, used to be terribly hokey and schlock just five or so years ago, and Fisherman's Wharf, to the natives was another name for tourist trap. The area, though, has dressed itself up and you don't immediately think you're being taken just by walking down the street. The shops have changed, the attractions have changed, and it has all melded into a magic place for children.

Before we get into the other attractions, let us look at food. Fisherman's Wharf restaurants are visited by natives and tourists alike because some of the best sea-food restaurants in the city are here. They are not overpoweringly expensive, but they are not cheap. Look at the menus posted on the front doors of the restaurants before you go in. On the sidewalks, you'll find stands selling crabs (fresh-steamed in season, frozen fresh-steamed out of season), fish of all sorts, walkaway sea-food cocktails, and San Francisco sour-dough French bread. Sour-dough bread is truly a specialty of San Francisco; you'll get it nowhere else. It's made only of flour, salt, and yeast, and it's the yeast that is special. In the old mining days, there was no handy supply of yeast to leaven the bread. They mixed the flour, salt, and water and set it out to let the native yeast cells in the air "start" the dough (that is, begin the fermenting, "souring" process that changes the starch in wheat flour to sugar, then carbon dioxide, which makes the little holes in a raised bread). They'd save some of today's bread batch, called the "mother," to begin the next day's mixing. That is how San Francisco's sour-dough bread is baked today. Attempts have been made to export our own peculiar yeast strain and "mother" to other places so the delicious bread could be baked commercially elsewhere, but it hasn't worked. There is something about San Francisco's climate or peculiar sea-level condition and temperature (even maybe mystical vibrations) that makes it impossible to duplicate our sour-dough bread anywhere else. The bread is as unique as our cables; you'll find it only here, so enjoy it while you can. It might be remembered that the sour-dough French bread found on Fisherman's Wharf is the same that you'll find in every grocery store in the city. There's no need to pay the premium price down there.

At this end of Fisherman's Wharf, there are many attractions: two wax museums, Ripley's Believe It or Not, a "Visit to Old San Francisco," many shops that sell Alcatraz convicts' hats with "Wish You Were Here" stamped on the top, and things like that. These things are as good as any you'll find in other Fisherman's Wharves along the coast but there *are* three tourist attractions you shouldn't miss while you're on this end of Fisherman's Wharf—perhaps four. As I said, this is a working wharf and there are several authentic deep-sea fishing and deep-water gear shops scattered among the souvenir shops. Go in and look around. You rarely see this kind of rugged sport and nautical stuff (such as various pumps, fishing floats, lures, crab and shrimp nets, cordage and needles for making your own nets). The ship's chandler shops (see page 213) have even more exotic merchandise, but you should look in here while you're on the Wharf. The three things you shouldn't miss are:

Harbor Tours.

At Pier 43½ is the fleet of Bay Cruise ships that give the second-best sightseeing bargain to be found in the city (the first is the ferries to Sausalito and Tiburon). These tours are hour-and-a-half cruises on the Bay under both the Golden Gate Bridge and the Bay Bridge, passing near Alcatraz and Angel Island, the captain giving a running account of what you're seeing on either side of the boat. It's a great experience for kids; it's safe and fun. I'm not usually given to recommending a commercial tourist enterprise, but this is very fine. The ships leave about every half-hour from 10:00 AM until dark in the summer and the price at this writing is $2.50 for adults; $1.00 for children 5–11; and under 5 free. My parents, in their sixties and seventies, took the cruise every time they visited us, and my little boy has done it at least five times and is eager to go again—it's that kind of good thing to do and enjoy.

Between Pier 43½ and the *Balclutha* is PIER 43, one of the two Southern Pacific train-ferry loading docks. If you're lucky, you'll be able to watch them load the boxcars on the train ferry.

The BALCLUTHA at Pier 43 might throw you off for a moment, because it looks tourist-hokey. You see this three-masted square-rigger advertised with garish signs and get the feeling that it's a shuck. It's not at all. This is one of the few opportunities in the world to visit a Round-the-Horn, working sailing ship. It was built at the turn of the century and boasts a trim hull-to-sail ratio that was one of the best in the history of sailing (the clipper ship *Cutty Sark* had a better ratio, but not too much better). The San Francisco Maritime Museum and wealthy patrons rescued the hulk from its end as an Alaskan cod-fisheries ship and, through donations, began a restoration project that has resulted in the largest floating museum in the world; the museum ship being itself a museum piece. Part of the donations came from one of the strangest sources to be found anywhere. The *Balclutha* was a pet project of the late Alma Spreckels (of the Hawaiian sugar fortune) and as a fund-raiser, she converted the carriage house of her mansion into a salvage shop (in other towns they're called thrift shops or second-hand stores), collecting sellables from rich friends and selling them at low prices. This salvage shop, housed in a piece of property on Pacific Heights, is worth at least a million in itself, and the success of the strange venture—the ultra-rich going into the old-clothes and used-furniture business—has been so great that it has been copied widely, to the point where fund-raisers from other cities have come to study the operation.

"Museum," according to the dictionary, means a place where objects of lasting worth or interest are displayed. It's interesting that this special museum was largely reconstructed by funds gotten from the wealthy selling their own small items of worth and interest, a family sofa, a Spanish comb, a few yards of lace that didn't get incorporated into a dress, silverware, an end table that had been in the family for years, bespoken men's suits and women's out-of-fashion dresses. Family museum pieces resurrected this fine ship. Alma Spreckels' salvage shop is still operating at Jackson and Gough Streets as the Patrons of Art and Music Salvage Shop. There are fine bargains to be had there.

The *Balclutha* is a unique place. For the rather modest tariff ($1.25 for adults; 65¢ for ages 12–17; 35¢ for children 6-12; children under 6 free with parents), you get a feeling unlike that of any other museum in the world. When you walk on the broad teak decks, you get an instant understanding of little bits and pieces half-remembered from stories about sailing ships. The main deck, for example, isn't flat like a floor. It's gently bent to shed the water, and it makes you walk like an old salt (and understand the description "a sailor's rolling gait"). This ship was on the high seas for months at a time on the run around the Horn, so you can see how the gait could become a habit. Again, the separation of the crew (who were "before the mast" men-of-all-work, but little specialization) and the elite of the crew and ships officers is finally understood, graphically. The common sailors were hired for their muscles, and stowed like cargo in the forecastle. Andrew Furuseth, the "Emancipator of Seamen," the first to organize the sailors into a labor union, said something like, "You can put me in jail, but the quarters will be no narrower than those I have always had as a seaman. . . ." You can see what he was talking about here. As you rose up the scale of skill in the trade, you were allotted more space and privacy—but the skill had to be there. The ship's carpenter, for example, had to know not only how to splice a mast when it blew down in a storm, but also cabinetmaking and veneering to embellish the captain's cabin in his spare time. The sumptuous captain's quarters are a revelation. From the descriptions in sailing-ship books, and from movies, you would think they were elegant, stately mansions. But the *Balclutha* is a good-sized ship and here you see that the space for the captain was only about as large as a smallish motel room, with lower ceilings. He had room enough to turn around in, and not much more. In comparison to the crew's quarters, he enjoyed the equivalent of a forty-acre farm. But the operation of these ships was not romantic or frivolous. Sailing the floating warehouse was a business. Anything that detracted from the space available to haul cargo was an unfortunate expense and kept to the minimum.

When you look at the details, you realize that going down to the sea in ships was a rather mean business for all concerned. But when you stand on the deck and look up through the rigging and feel the ship move beneath your feet, you understand the romance and affection and nostalgia that sailors have always felt. A sailing ship is an infinitely complicated piece of equipment. Getting from New York to California or Australia by sail was a chancy task involving scientific know-how, practical seamanship, lots of hard work hauling in and putting out the sails, the luck of good or bad winds, the luck of storms and reefs, self-reliance within the confines of the ship on the ocean. In other words, it was a great job to work at. The living conditions were terrible for all concerned, but the job was great. No wonder so many men forsook good living conditions to take to the sea. It is something kids understand instantly when they go aboard the *Balclutha*.

There are three deck levels of museum treasures here, large and small. Included in the entrance price is a carry-around talking-tour device that will explain the ship as you move from point to point. If you have to skip another San Francisco attraction to see this, don't hesitate. A good sequence of looking at things in the Fisherman's Wharf area is to walk through the Maritime Museum, visit the smaller coastal ships at the San Francisco Maritime State Historic Park, then tour the *Balclutha.*

Near the *Balclutha* is a new attraction, a *helicopter tour* of the Bay. I almost hesitate to include it because it too smacks of a "tourist gimmick." It's expensive, at this writing $5 per person, and the helicopter ride is short, averaging about four minutes. It does, though, let you experience a helicopter ride and a wonderful view of the bridges and the Bay. If you've never been on a helicopter and always wanted to, you'll get your money's worth. I have never ridden it because I'm not that fond of flying in anything. It's there, though, and on the positive side, if you don't fool your money away on this, it will be spent on something else. Those who come off the helicopter are smiling.

Between the *Balclutha* and the helicopter is the TIBURON–ANGEL ISLAND FERRYBOAT. This (along with the SAUSALITO FERRYBOAT) is one of the great tourist bargains in San Francisco. They were both brought into being to answer the problem of auto congestion on the Golden Gate Bridge. By 1975, there will be more ferry systems with bigger boats. Primarily services for commuters, they are also great boat rides on the Bay, and cheap.

There are three ferry rides; to Tiburon, to Angel Island, and to Sausalito. They are all excellent rides, shorter than the Harbor Tours Guided Bay Tour and they offer no description of the things you are seeing, but they're fine adventures.

The ferry to Tiburon leaves from here on weekends and holidays at 10 AM, 12 noon, 2 PM, and 3:45 PM. It leaves Tiburon at 11 AM, 1 PM, 2:50 PM, and 4:20 PM. The price at this writing is 75¢ for adults, 25¢ for children 6–12—these are one-way fares. Check both the times and fares when you want to take the boats— they're subject to change. During the week, commuter ferries leave from the Ferry Building to Tiburon at 7:30 AM, 4 PM, 5:15 PM, and 5:45 PM. They return from Tiburon to the Ferry Building at 6:30 AM, 7:30 AM, 8:10 AM, and 6:30 PM; to Fisherman's Wharf at 4:45, 5:55, and 8 PM.

Now, 75¢ for a half-hour boat ride on the Bay is certainly a great bargain, but once you get to either Tiburon or Sausalito, you find that you're in good places as well.

TIBURON is a rich little town on the Belvedere–Tiburon peninsula, once a site for "country homes" for the very rich. There are yacht clubs, extremely fine houses, and a main shopping street full of specialty shops. A special treat in Tiburon is a hamburger at Sam's. From the street, Sam's looks like a rather grungy bar, but once you have passed through the bar to the deck on the Bay, you'll find it delightful. Here are loads of tables overlooking the yacht harbor and a beautiful view of San Francisco. The clientele is international and they don't mind children. Tourists from all over the world come to enjoy the view, the sun on Sam's desk, and Sam's famous hamburgers and Ramos Fizzes. They serve complete meals from an extensive menu, but the hamburgers are special: huge, excellent, and surprisingly inexpensive. Sam's Ramos Fizzes are a delicious concoction of gin, frothed egg white, cream, and juices but they are, of course, for adults only. There are soft drinks and juices for the kids. There are other deck restaurants in Tiburon, but Sam's is my favorite. While waiting for the ferry back (after looking through the shops), you'll find a kind of penny arcade, with antique music and games machines, conveniently near the ferry dock. Both kids and adults find it interesting.

The ferryboat to Angel Island also leaves from the Fisherman's Wharf ferry slip where the Tiburon ferry docks. Round trip, it's $1.75 for adults and 75¢ for children five to eleven. It leaves San Francisco on

Saturdays, Sundays, and holidays at 10 AM, noon, and 2 PM; returning from Angel Island at 12:45, 2:35, and 4:35 PM (check all these times before you go down).

ANGEL ISLAND is a state park and slated to become part of the proposed Coast and Bay National Parks complex (various city, state, and national parklands and holdings along the ocean joined together under National Park supervision). It's a rather wild and charming island that has long been a favorite picnic and hiking spot for Bay Area families. One of the most interesting islands in the Bay, it has a very curious history. At various times, it has been a Coast Guard station; the site of several Army camps; a Nike missile site, and the Ellis Island of the West, where immigrants from the Orient were quarantined before going on to the mainland. Today, the island is largely wilderness area (semitame deer abound) and is being opened up more and more every year. For many years, the crumbling buildings were too dangerous for visitors and large chunks of the island were off limits. An elephant-train tour of the island shows the various compounds and includes a lecture on the history of the island.

ALCATRAZ The boat for the Alcatraz tour also leaves from pier 41½; tickets are at the Tiburon ticket office. The facilities and manpower of the government park service are as yet limited, and only fifty people are permitted per one hour tour. *You must* call 398–1141 for reservations for the tour, and good luck. At this writing (four months after the tour started) I have not been able to book space. I understand, though, that the tour is very interesting and worth a good try.

SAUSALITO is another thing entirely. A former fishing village that has turned into a haven for artists and craftsmen (bohemian, but expensive), Sausalito is a lovely little town to walk through and has some of the finest shops in the Bay Area. Gourmet restaurants are found in numbers all out of proportion to the size of the town. The Sausalito ferry leaves from its dock between Pier 1 and the Ferry Building. There are ten departures from San Francisco from 7:50 AM to 8:10 PM on weekdays, roughly every hour. There are eleven departures from Sausalito, starting at 7:15 AM, 8:50 PM during the week. On Saturdays, Sundays, and holidays, the present schedule has ferries leaving at 10:25 AM, 11:45 AM, 1:15 PM, 2:45 PM, 4:10 PM, 5:30 PM, and 6:50 PM. The boats leave Sausalito at 11:05 AM, 12:30 PM, 2 PM, 3:30 PM, 4:50 PM, 6:10 PM, and 7:30 PM. The price is 75¢ one way for adults, 25¢ for children six to twelve.

Be careful of the schedules on all these ferry trips, especially the last-boat times from Sausalito and the other points. If you miss the last ferry, you'll have to come back by bus or taxi (the first, inconvenient; the second, expensive). I don't know what happens to the people who miss the last ferry from Angel Island, because you can't walk home from there.

How to Drive to Fisherman's Wharf

If you don't want to take the cable cars—or plan to go on from Fisherman's Wharf to other attractions, here are three of the best routes to Fisherman's Wharf from Union Square.

1. Drive out Geary to Van Ness Avenue and turn right. Follow Van Ness to its end at the Bay. At the foot of Van Ness, you're at Aquatic Park near the Maritime Museum and Ghirardelli Square, and the west end of Fisherman's Wharf. There's public parking on the street, usually. If no parking is available there, retrace up the hill to the first street to your left (North Point) and use the parking garage at Ghirardelli Square. If that one is full there are several other parking garages in the neighborhood.

2. Drive out Geary two blocks to Taylor Street and right up the hill. This is an extremely steep hill, so if you're chicken, drive two more blocks to Leavenworth and turn right there. In either case, turn right on

California Street to Mason Street (you'll pass Grace Cathedral: the two hotels on the corner are the Fairmont and the Mark Hopkins). Turn left on Mason. Follow Mason all the way down to Bay Street where there is parking in the Akron lot. If that's full, keep going a couple of blocks to Jefferson. There is usually metered parking around this area. If you can't find a place, there are several lots in the neighborhood. In the summer at midday, it's murder trying to find a parking space. That's why I suggest the cable cars.

3. Head right up the Powell Street hill, following the cable car tracks, and keep on Powell to Broadway. Here, you're near Chinatown, North Beach, and the nightclub area. Turn right on Broadway to the Embarcadero. To your left is Fisherman's Wharf, to your right is the Ferry Building and the Sausalito Ferry. Public parking is available on Pier 1 if you want the ferry ride to Sausalito. If you turn left to the Fisherman's Wharf area, you can sometimes find metered parking a couple of short blocks from Fisherman's Wharf on the Embarcadero.

3

Golden Gate Park

Driving: Out Geary Street to Masonic Avenue (the big Sears Roebuck store is to your left). Turn left onto Masonic. Keep in the right lane down the hill to Fell Street which is One Way to your right. Turn right on Fell and proceed to the park's main entrance.

Public Transportation: Catch the No. 5 McAllister Street bus, which skirts the Park on the north. Tenth Avenue is the entrance to the Music Concourse and the main attractions. The N Judah streetcar line runs a block or two to the south of the Park. Get off at Ninth Avenue to reach the main attractions. Both these lines are boarded on Market Street and both go all the way to the Pacific Ocean on either side of the Park.

Golden Gate Park is an incredible place. The most amazing thing about the park is not a listing of its many wonders but the fact of the park itself. It seems impossible to believe, when you are looking at it now, that this grand park was once a desolation of sand dunes, but it's true. From Stanyan Street to the ocean, this whole area of town was a wasteland—so much so that the early maps labeled this part of San Francisco "uninhabitable." What now is lush greenery was all created artificially. Every tree, every bush, every blade of grass was planted by the hand of man. It's one of the largest man-made "natural" city parks in the world.

The park is three miles long (not including the Panhandle) and half a mile wide. The variety of attractions it contains seems almost endless. From children's playgrounds to the largest collection of Oriental art in America; from exotic sea creatures to a lake where you can rent rowboats; from horseshoe courts to lawn-bowling greens, there is something here for everyone. Surprisingly, the attractions that seem mainly geared to adults with specialized interests, such as the rose, camellia, fuchsia, and tulip gardens (hundreds of exotic varieties), appeal to children as well because they are close to areas where the kids can run or climb trees or play Frisbee. There are some features in the park that are major tourist attractions of San Francisco and should not be missed. There are other attractions that are fun to visit and will let you (and your kids) relax from touring. Because there are so many things to see, and each family has its own interests, I'll begin at the main entrance of the park at Fell and Stanyan Streets and describe each section and attraction in order as we progress to the other end of the park. You'll be able to sort out what interests you and what you'll want to save for a later trip.

Motor traffic is allowed through the park every day but Sunday; then the main area is open only to pedestrians and bicycles (and horses and roller skates). To tell you the truth, the bicyclers who zip around on the carless roads on Sundays are almost as much a menace as the cars—although getting run down by a careless ten-speeder isn't like getting run over by a car. You can rent your own bicycles from several shops along Stanyan Street near the park entrance; from Fulton Street on the north side of the park and Lincoln Way on the south side of the park, around both Ninth and Tenth Avenues. (Both of these are mobile outfits so their location isn't permanent, but can be found near those main entrances), and again on Lincoln Way near the far end of the park around Forty-seventh Avenue. The hourly rates are very reasonable; a small deposit is required.

A new feature has been added to the park recently —the shuttle buses that leave from McLaren Lodge near Stanyan Street and travel to the main attractions of the park. One ticket is good all day, and you can get off at any point and reboard the bus when you want to travel farther.

As you enter the park, the park headquarters, McLaren Lodge, is to your right. It's named for John McLaren, "The Father of Golden Gate Park," who was the park superintendant for most of the park's history. It was he who turned the sand dunes into a garden spot. McLaren was a single-minded, dedicated, crusty old Scotsman who gained so much affection in the eyes of his fellow San Franciscans that anything he said went. William Hammond Hall, who laid out New York's Central Park, laid out Golden Gate Park. McLaren made it green with grass and trees (after much experimentation and hard work). Of course, when it became a beauty spot, the politicians tried to take it over, finding it the most perfect spot in the city to put up buildings and statues and stadiums. McLaren's philosophy was simple. A huge amount of money, worry, effort, time, and planning had gone into creating trees, grass, bushes, and flowers on the sand dunes. Why rip out these painstakingly grown "natural" things to put up buildings, statues, and stadiums that could just as well be put somewhere else? It became a running battle, with the majority of the people on McLaren's side. His special peeve was statues, in an age that was statue and monument happy. He called them "stookies." Everybody wanted to "embellish" the park with his own favorite statue. McLaren's opposition kept most of them out and those he couldn't block by political muscle, he handled by his own kind of botanical warfare. The Scots-

Irish, for example, commissioned a statue of Robert Burns and put it up about opposite the Conservatory. McLaren immediately planted bushes around it so that it was effectively hidden unless you were standing directly in front of it. You'll see many statues along the main drive (John F. Kennedy Drive) that peer out through veritable tunnels of vegetation planted by McLaren. He was a good man and his philosophy has so endured that the trees and grass of Golden Gate Park have remained largely "natural." The citizens have turned down bad things, such as the plan to put a freeway through part of the park, and good things as well. Recently a bequest of nearly a million dollars was left to build a senior citizen's center in Golden Gate Park. There couldn't be a finer cause than that, but it was reluctantly turned down. Every cause is worth while, but if each worth-while cause chipped away a little piece of the park, soon the park would be gone. What we have here is a unique place where people can walk in the woods in a city that packs twenty thousand people per square mile; and kids can climb trees and play Cowboys and Indians in the bushes.

At McLaren Lodge, you can get all the information you want about Golden Gate Park. It's a city office, open Monday–Friday, 8 AM–5 PM, closed on weekends and holidays.

The Conservatory

Just beyond McLaren Lodge to your right is the Conservatory. It's a copy of the Kew Gardens conservatory, donated to the city by James Lick, the same man who donated so many fine things to the people, such as the Lick Observatory on Mount Hamilton. This is a curious place surrounded by curious things. The Conservatory itself is full of tropical and semitropical plants—some so smacking of science fiction that they look as though they'll eat you. It's rather a serious place showing the results of dedicated exotic gardening, but also the kind of place where there are some good things for all ages. If you garden or are interested in indoor plants you will gain heart when you see what your efforts *could* become. Little kids can climb the bridges over the pool in the east wing and look at the huge goldfish. Seven-to-twelvers get knocked right in the eye when they enter. Under the main rotunda are the "man-eaters" (I know *I* don't get too close to them) and great plants with leaves that are big enough to make a *tent* out of. Here also are banana plants that show that bananas don't grow downward, as you might expect, but turn up, like your fingers with your palm up. In the west wing there is usually a changing display of exotic flowers such as tuberous begonias and orchids. It's a painlessly educational place to go.

Outside, to your right and up the hill, are the camellia and fuchsia gardens. The two main points of interest are the floral clock and the floral plaque. The clock was a gift to the city from the Swiss watchmakers. The floral plaque is an unique art form. The subject changes with the sponsors—there is a fairly large fee for advertising here. All the colors come from living plants and they must be planted in a precise way so the design on the sloping ground near the Conservatory appears normal when seen from the main drive. From the road it appears as flat as a picture in a frame; from close up, it's a little bent to compensate for the distortion. It takes skill and time to set the plants and the park charges for it.

Children's Playground and Near It

Approximately across the street from the Conservatory is a road leading to your left to the Children's Playground, tennis courts, and lawn-bowling greens.

This is a fine place to offer low-key release for a group of children of mixed ages.

The CHILDREN'S PLAYGROUND has a wide variety of facilities for letting off steam. Toddlers and pre-schoolers can romp in sand piles, slide down really great slides, or go on the finest merry-go-round in the city. There is a small "farm" here where you can pet the ducks, pigs, goats, sheep, and an occasional llama. Kids a little older can climb on (and jump from) an old cable car, try even more wild slides, or practice gymnastics on the hanging rings, parallel bars, and vaulting horses (there are usually a few high-schoolers who work out here in the afternoons). While the little kids play, the teen-agers can walk over to the LAWN-BOWLING GREENS and watch a sport seldom seen in America. Lawn bowling is a wonderful sport in which one rolls biased balls (flattened a little) in curving arcs toward the small object ball (called the "jack"). It would be popular all over except for the care and maintainence of the green. Here, the greens can be used all year—we have no snow or freezing weather.

The TENNIS COURTS are also of interest because, being among the best in the city, they attract excellent players. If your kids are interested in tennis, they will probably like to watch these players, or watch the resident tennis pro give lessons.

There is a snack bar at the Children's Playground that sells hot dogs, popcorn, soft drinks, and ice cream. Touring is tough on kids. They have to sit still too long and stay too clean and are strangers on a new turf. Here, they can wind down a little and the parents can sit on sun-warmed benches and relax for a bit. The Children's Playground is in a lovely setting and you'll have all the varieties of folks in the world sitting next to you on the benches. It's a good breathing spot and an hour away from your schedule can do wonders for the rest of your visit.

The Music Concourse Area

Here is the main cultural center of Golden Gate Park, and a major cultural center for the city. The De Young Museum (fine art); Center of Asian Art and Culture (Oriental fine art); the California Academy of Sciences (Planetarium, Aquarium, Natural History Museum); the Japanese Tea Garden; the McLaren Memorial Rhododendron Dell; the Arboretum, and Stow Lake are all within a short walk of each other and are of interest to the whole family.

Depending on the family, some parts are of more interest than others and the interest range is broad. Parking is available on the south side of the Concourse. If that's full, go past the De Young, turn left past the Band Shell and left again following the parking arrows. Parking is murder in the summer, but you can usually find a place behind the Aquarium or on Lincoln Way. It involves only a short walk and, once you see the Concourse, you can find your way back.

THE DE YOUNG MUSEUM. Daily, 10 AM–5 PM. Free. This is the "official" museum of the city, even though we have two other major museums. Any major exhibits touring the country (and showing in San Francisco) will be shown here—such as the Van Gogh collection, the Norman Rockwell collection, and the collection of Eskimo art. It's not as rich and well-endowed as many other major city museums, but if your kids have never seen an authentic Old Master in the flesh, they will be able to see one here. My seven-year old doesn't quite believe that these paintings are artistic or even antique, but he likes the small selection of Egyptian, Greek, and Roman antiquities. Be prepared to answer "How did he die?" when you get to the mummy. Here you can strike a blow: "His daddy told him not to play in the street and he got run over by a chariot," or "He only ate candy and junk instead of good food and he got sick and died." They're at least as good as "I don't know." There are some suits of armor and antique swords, pistols, and chain mail that boys will find interesting, and complete restored rooms from various periods that should interest teen-agers with a little history under their belts. Of special interest to kids are the native culture displays of the arts and crafts of Indians, Polynesians, and Africans.

SAN FRANCISCO CENTER OF ASIAN ART AND CULTURE. Adjoins the De Young, same hours.

This is the Avery Brundage collection of Asian art and artifacts. Also for older kids also. It is the finest collection of Asian art in America (a $30-million value has been assigned) and is a unique experience. Brundage, the sometimes-crusty director of the Olympic Games, has honored this city with his stupendous collection of every aspect of Asian art. Here you'll see with your own eyes the things that usually are seen only in fine-art books about some aspect of Asian art. Kids like the antiquity of the pieces and the fact that most of the exhibits are fine craft stuff (statues, castings, bas-relief carvings, pottery, jewelry) instead of Western fine art, which runs mostly to paintings and monumental sculpture. Little kids would prefer to play around the fountain on the ground floor instead of looking at any of it—and they do. Fortunately, there are good places nearby where one adult can take the little ones while the other enjoys the collection in peace; then trade off.

CALIFORNIA ACADEMY OF SCIENCES. Opposite the De Young. Daily, 10 AM–5 PM (9 PM in summer). There is a modest admission charge. First Saturday of every month free.

This is definitely a family place and one of the most popular attractions in the city. More people visited the Academy last year than visited the Louvre. It's a complex of four buildings, each containing a wealth of experience and good things to look at, and it's always expanding. There is a special charm about this place, an excitement in just passing through.

You walk in the door and are confronted by the largest dinosaur skeleton to be seen west of the Mississippi. There are usually two special exhibits in this hall (and two gift shops. A cafeteria is downstairs in this new wing).

To your right is the North American Hall. Immediately inside to your right is a small but elegant butterfly collection. North American Hall is devoted to an exhibit of large American land and sea mammals. Now, a collection of stuffed animals immediately brings all kinds of questions. The little kids ask, "Are they dead?"; the older kids say, "What are we looking at dead stuff for?" and, from the teen-agers, you'll get, "How could they kill these endangered species?" The answers are: "Yes they are dead"; "This is as close to an elk or moose or sea elephant as you're ever likely to get, living or dead"; and, "Most of these beasts were collected when there appeared to be a danger that they would be wiped out before the average person could see them close up—not in a painting or photograph." They are all displayed in a setting as close to their natural habitat as painstaking naturalists could make them. This museum was the first in the world to display animals this way, a method since copied everywhere. And if it's a little lugubrious to see case after case of dead, stuffed animals, you can point out to your kids that, here, you can get an idea of how big the animals really were—photographs don't really show that. Man, the hunter-gatherer, stalked and killed these beasts with spear and bow and arrow. Looking at them in their wild setting, ask your kids if they could sneak up through the terrain they see and kill them for food. When you see how big they really are (man is one of the largest carni-vores on earth), ask how long a deer or moose would feed a band of hunting men and their families; how they would preserve the meat they couldn't eat on the spot; and, considering that all the implements necessary to skag these beasts—the spear and arrow points, the seasoned wood for bows, arrows, and spears—had to be made by hand, exactly how much work went into getting something for the dinner table —or campfire? The North American Hall is not just a collection of stuffed animals.

Passing through the North American Hall, you come to a hall of specimen birds. Of great interest are the sea-bird exhibits. You may examine these close at hand, something rarely permitted in the field. For the inlander, this will be the only chance to view these sea birds at all, dead or alive. Again, such a large display of stuffed animals, birds in this case, tends to depress, but the purpose is to educate yourself. You can examine all these birds minutely, studying the length of beak, color of the feathers, type of feet and claws. Unless you kill your own or capture a little one and raise it, you'll never have a closer look at a rare bird.

The Mineral Hall, in this wing, displays museum-quality examples of crystals, ores, and geologic won-ders from all over the world. These are very fine and make rockhounds gnash their teeth in envy (see Chapter 10 for another fine display). Three exhibits here are especially interesting to children. One is the fluorescent rock display in the middle of the corridor. It's built so that little kids can peer through windows on the side or climb on top of it and look down. Under normal light, you see just rocks. When the ultra-violet light hits them, they glow and sparkle in great gaudy colors. The second is a very fine pushbutton earthquake-explaining model. It shows how the earth moves along fault lines and how mountains are made. The third is a working seismograph. The most recent earthquakes are shown on a tear sheet from the moving graph paper and displayed above the seismograph. While you watch it, you can see the pen flow along smoothly, then give a couple of little bumps which record an earthquake halfway around the world. It's funny, but when you look at it, you hope that an earthquake will hit San Francisco just so you can see the pen jump. The pen records time by a steep dip evey minute. When you see the pen-line drop, you tend to touch the side of the building to see if you are in a real earthquake right now.

There is a small room between the birds and the Aquarium devoted to Paleolithic things—mastodon, ancient whales, fish and dinosaur bones. In a well-like display that shows how paleontologists dig the history of animals from the earth, there are bones shown *in situ*, like the La Brea exhibit in Los Angeles.

STEINHART AQUARIUM. Continuing, you come to one of the finest aquariums in the world and one of the main reasons the Academy of Sciences is so popular. You're nose to nose with an incredible display of fish and aquatic mammals. There's everything here from fresh-water trout to tropic octopus; from dolphins in a huge tank with seals and sea birds through sharks and alligator gars to a tide-pool tank that splashes water upon sea anemones. You'll find a manatee and piranhas, sea turtles and bluegills. From Marineland in Miami to Marine World down the coast in San Mateo county, nothing equals this. It's great fun to go with kids. Two-year-olds, who have an interest span of perhaps five minutes in any other kind of exhibit—even their toes—will gleefully drag you from fish tank to fish tank and cry when it's time to go. At the courtyard entrance to the Aquarium is a sunken pool full of crocodiles, alligators, and turtles. For some reason, there is a strange compulsion to toss money into sunken pools, fountains, and wells. If you've ever wished upon a star, here's your chance to wish upon an alligator. In back of the saurian grotto, in a semicircle, are exhibits of lizards, amphibians, and snakes—all exotic and a great many deadly poisonous or capable of crushing small children. Naturally, this is a grand point of interest.

As good as it is, the Steinhart Aquarium will soon be even better. An addition is planned in the back of the building—a great circular tank that will expand the facilities greatly. The place is such a fine thing now, it will be exciting to see what greater wonders we'll find here in the future.

Continuing around the Academy, you pass from the Aquarium immediately into outer space. When you leave the Aquarium, you'll see an exhibit of meteorites, and scales that will give you your weight when you're on the moon and a pendulum that illustrates the rotation of the earth. This wing holds the MORRISON PLANETARIUM which is a must. There is a modest charge, but the experience is unforgettable. Outside it's daylight and inside, all of a sudden, it's deepest night, with millions of stars. This star projector was the first in America (the Academy has a lot of firsts to its credit, considering its size). Because these planetariums are few and far between, check on the next showing when you enter the Academy and buy your tickets right away. It's extremely popular and might be sold out for an entire afternoon. A visit to any planetarium is basically a popular science-lecture with slides—a modern magic-lantern show. The difference is in the drama. The stars blaze above you as if you were high in the mountains. The lecture is given, with comets, or planets, or double stars, or whatever, while you're seated in total darkness. The sun finally rises at the end and you go out into daylight once again. That's an experience!

There are two other exhibits in this hall, one of the history of time keeping (all kinds of clocks) and the other of how man illuminated his home before electricity and the electric light. There is a tendency to pass them by because they are specialized, but stop and look at them.

Of all the animals, man alone has fussed with, "What time is it?" Ask your kids, "If you didn't have a watch, how could you measure something so nebulous as 'time'"? Here you'll see water clocks and candle clocks, sundials and pendulums, spring and electric clocks and watches. Time is invisible and it's a tribute to man's genius that he has felt compelled to make one machine after another so that he can say, "Right now, it's a quarter to twelve!" A family sundial is a great project after you see this exhibit (it will give you the exact sun time exactly where you are instead of fuzzy agreed-upon time for your particular time zone—a good feeling for some reason).

The ancient-lamps exhibit is even more interesting, if for no other reason than that these lamps are not all that ancient. Electric light is brand-new. As late as the 1930's, many farms were without electricity (remember the Rural Electrification Project?). Kerosene and coal-oil lamps aren't that much older, though those lamps are "antique" now. Lighting by natural gas and petroleum products is a relatively new development—Lincoln didn't know them as a boy. All interior lighting not so long ago was furnished by candles or by burning animal or vegetable fats in the kinds of lamps you see here. Everybody knows the charm of candlelight, but it's interesting to see what other kind of lighting people had before petroleum and electricity. Whether they burned olive oil (in the Middle East), seal fat (Far North), tallow, pork fat, whale oil (in Europe and America), it all entailed putting a cloth or vegetable wick into some kind of oil and lighting it. This is another good family project and will give your kids a concrete example of how it was at night in the "olden times." Try it with a small ash tray, a piece of cotton clothesline or heavy string, and some olive oil—or any cooking oil, salad oil, or lard. Open the windows when you do it at home because if the wick isn't properly positioned, it's smoky and it smells.

A hall just beyond the Morrison Planetarium is used for temporary exhibits; at this writing it's devoted to an exhibition of American Indian artifacts. Just beyond that is a small hall devoted to botany, then there is an additional Space section with an eight-foot illuminated model of the moon. The African Hall, with stuffed animals of that continent, again in their natural habitats, follows, and you are again at the entrance.

There is a cafeteria in the Academy, as well as four gift counters where you may buy exotic sea shells, mineral specimens, or books. The counter near the Planetarium has a few telescope mirror blanks so you can grind your own. Lots of postcards are available and some great posters.

THE MUSIC CONCOURSE. Between the De Young and the Academy of Sciences is a sunken auditorium with fountains and a band shell. On Sundays, at 2 PM, you may enjoy free concerts presented by either the Municipal Band or one of the many, many ethnic societies in the city. You're apt to find anything there on Sunday afternoon, from a Lithuanian National Day Celebration, to Guatamalan festivals, to Irish jigs, to rock bands. All is free and you may be sure that the kids will stop you to see, even if you're not too interested yourself.

JAPANESE TEA GARDEN. Just to the west of the De Young, a short way beyond the band shell, is one of the most charming attractions of the park. It's for both children and adults in that, though the whole layout of the Japanese Tea Garden is an expression of the skill and expertise of Japanese landscaping, design, and artistic horticulture, there are also features within it that will thrill the kids. If you have problems of what to do with that corner of your back yard, you can examine what these clever gardeners have done while the kids haul themselves up the cleats of the Moon Bridge (it's shaped like an upside down letter "U" and it's probably the only bridge you'll ever see that you have to *climb* over), look at the goldfish in the pools, or feed the tame squirrels. There is an outdoor tea garden (and gift shop) in the middle of the Tea Garden where kimonoed Japanese waitresses serve regular or jasmine tea and tiny rice crackers and cookies. The wildmen you couldn't drag away from the Moon Bridge magically transform themselves into decent citizens because they're drinking real tea from little cups without handles, with the china teapot on the table, and opening fortune cookies. Everybody likes the Japanese Tea Garden.

STOW LAKE. If you're parked and near the Japanese Tea Garden, go out the back gate and up the flight of stairs to Stow Lake. It's not a major attraction but a very pleasant circular lake that surrounds Strawberry Hill, the highest point in the park. Here are rowboats, paddle boats, and electric motorboats for hire (as well as a snack bar). Lots of ducks, walkers, and joggers. It's a beautiful lake and the climb up Strawberry Hill will give you a wonderful western view of the city and the Pacific Ocean.

THE ARBORETUM. At the Ninth Avenue entrance to the park from Lincoln Way. There are a lot of good things here for adults and for older kids who have an interest in botany. It's a forty-acre park within Golden Gate Park, full of exotic plants, trees, and shrubs. There are some five thousand different varieties of plant life representing every continent and nearly every country in the world. If you're at the Music Concourse, go past the band shell and turn left at the first road (about a block). There is an information booth near the entrance that will give you the plan of the place.

The special features that the adults might want to visit are the *Sunset* magazine display of what to do with your garden or patio. There must be twenty different kinds of paving alone, from brick to river pebbles. The Garden of Fragrance is interesting. It's planted especially for the blind, and all the plants have been selected for their own special taste, smell, or feel. The plants are at touch level and are described in written letters and in Braille.

These are the major attractions in the most-visited area of the park around the Music Concourse. For the most part, they are family things. Farther out, though, Golden Gate Park offers many special delights that add spice to any visit.

The Spreckels Lake Area

As you continue out John F. Kennedy Drive, you'll pass Rainbow Falls. Perched atop it is Prayerbrook Cross, honoring the first Protestant service offered on the West Coast of North America by the Anglican chaplain of Sir Francis Drake's ship, which came ashore to scrape her bottom at Drake's Bay, thirty miles north of the city. The rocks beneath the waterfall have the finest Radiolaria specimens to be found on the West Coast.

You'll go under a bridge and past several meadows, and on your right you'll see SPRECKELS LAKE. The meadows to your left used to be used as a race course in the olden days—Speedway Meadows, they're called. The lake is used now as another kind of race course; it's shared by both model sailboats and model engine-driven boats—and seagulls and ducks. The model boats you will see here are the real thing. Every Saturday and Sunday, and sometimes during the week, you can see the members of the San Francisco Model Yacht Club exercising their crafts. Both the sail- and motorboats have been meticulously handcrafted and minutely finished to resemble full-scale boats—real boats. When you look at them, you wonder why people would spend so much time building these boats in the small when with the same amount of time and not too much more money, they could build them full scale—but these are model-builders, and they are a breed apart. The sailboats tack as though they're competing for the America's Cup; the motorboats, which include tug boats, steam boats, cabin cruisers, hydroplanes, and radio-controlled runabouts, blat around the lake as if each were *Miss Bardahl*. The motor craft are allowed to operate only before 1 PM, so if you want to see them, go to the park early.

Across from Spreckels Lake are the POLO FIELDS. There are riding stables there with horses for hire, but the field also offers entertainment most of the year around, and exotic entertainment indeed. In winter (approximately during the football season), there are regular rugby and lacrosse games to be seen. There used to be polo in the Polo Fields until two years ago, but the expense of keeping up the grounds was too great.

Regional amateur cross-country and track and field events are held on and near the Polo Fields (We will deal with these things more extensively in Chapter 25).

This whole area from Spreckels Lake to the ocean is spotted with interesting features. At the Fulton Street side of Spreckels Lake, go down the dirt road (literally down the hill—if you go up, you're headed in the wrong direction) a few hundred yards and you'll come to the DOG TRAINING FIELD (it's near the old Police Academy building, which is now a senior citizen's center). Here, at almost any time of the day, year around, you're apt to see people putting their dogs through the paces that are required in obedience trials in dog shows—dogs fetching dumbbells and leaping hurdles. The place is usually full of dogs with owners, but you rarely see them bark and snap at each other; even the neighborhood dogs who drop over regularly to check the action rarely cause a disturbance—perhaps because they realize it's a working place and not mere doggy foolishment. The joggers, who run along this road as part of a cross-country course, usually run with a handful of rocks because the neighborhood dogs consider them a moving target, but it's surprising how well behaved all the dogs are around here.

If you're interested in fly or plug casting, you'll see a sign on John F. Kennedy Drive near Spreckels Lake that says FISHERMAN'S LODGE. It's to the right-hand side of the Polo Field on the same side of the road and offers three casting pools with floating rings to test your accuracy. The people who use the casting pools are usually in training for some kind of competition, and you can try your hand yourself or watch a serious casting competitor whip a fly so that it lights in a two-foot ring fifty feet away. The Fisherman's Lodge usually has a few people who know about the local fishing prospects. Some joker has stocked the pools with trout, but I'm sure they're safe as aces. When you're practicing your casting, you don't want some fool fish to mess your line up.

Also near Spreckels Lake, farther toward the ocean, is the BUFFALO PADDOCK. It's a three-acre meadow with a friendly herd of buffalo and is an interesting place to stop with the kids. (Before you go to Golden Gate Park, be sure to buy a loaf of bread—the unsliced long-loaf French sour dough is the best because you can tear it into little pieces more easily. In every lake, there are ducks to feed and, here, the buffalo dote on sour-dough bread.) The Indians of the Plains hunted these huge buffalo on foot before the Spanish introduced horses to North America. The forequarters of the buffalo are burly and their hindquarters are as trim as those of a thoroughbred race horse. They must have been a formidable beast to attack on foot with a spear or bow and arrow. Even when the Indians had horses, the killing of the buffalo at a running gallop was a chancy thing. There are usually little buffalo calves to be seen. They look like cattle calves—with their heads a little too big. The buffalo come readily to the fence to eat bread from your hand and you can feel the wool around their head and shoulders. It's much finer than wool and feels almost like mohair. They graze on coarser pasture than cattle and there is talk of expanding the domestic herds in Western United States to capitalize on their hardiness, excellent by-products, and delicious meat. In San Francisco, you can look an American buffalo in the eye here and also eat buffalo stew at Tommy's Joynt (from commercial herds in Montana) on the corner of Van Ness and Geary.

On the road to the left at the end of the Buffalo Paddock is the EQUESTRIAN FIELD. People practice here for the various horse-handling techniques seen in county fairs and special meets. One may rent horses here also, or take guided horseback tours and hay rides.

As you go down John F. Kennedy Drive to the ocean, you'll find a nine-hole GOLF COURSE to your right and the soccer pitches to the left. If your family plays golf, I can say that it is an excellent course, but in the summer, don't count on getting to play on the spur of the moment. Call in advance for times on the course.

The SOCCER PITCHES on the left are another thing. In soccer, there is action, great exercise, and little of the head-to-head violence involved in football. Speed, agility, and endurance, plus teamwork, are paramount. In basketball, you dribble and pass with the hands; in soccer, you dribble with the feet, head, elbows—everything but the hands. Most Americans have never seen a good soccer game. In San Francisco, there are dozens of teams (nearly every Irish, English, European, Mexican, Central and South American social club fields is own *futbal* team) and at the soccer pitches, they practice for competitions at one of San Francisco's two soccer stadiums. There is no elaborate equipment involved—no helmets, shoulder pads, or whatever. All you really need is a big field, a ball, and people wanting to play.

The ARCHERY FIELDS are located almost at the beach —to your right on the road just past the nine-hole golf course. Everyone who has ever owned a bow and arrow set should go by there. Here, you're able to see the latest in space-age archery equipment—wrist triggers, stabilizing antennae, six-curve laminated wood-plastic-resin-metal-Fiberglass (and God knows what all) bows, and arrows that look as though they were calibrated in Cape Kennedy for perfect balance.

This brings us to the end of the park and the Pacific Ocean. There are two things to see here; one is a curiosity of nature and the other is a major tourist attraction of the city (which we will cover next). At the ocean side of the park, you'll see, all along the Great Highway, a planting of stunted, sandblasted trees so tortured by the constant wind that they flow in beautifully sculptured forms. Along this part of the coast, we seldom have kindly sea breezes; it's a wind and usually a stiff one and cold—stiff enough to sandpaper the bark and leaves from the windward side of these trees. They're Monterey cypress, a tree formerly found only along the roughest part of this exposed coastline. These trees are extremely tough and were deliberately planted to act as a windbreak for the next plantings in line in the park. As you entered the park at Stanyan Street you saw, on the lawn near McLaren Park, a magnificent one hundred-foot giant that is used as the official city Christmas tree (the Fire Department hook-and-ladder trucks decorate it every December). That is also a Monterey cypress. What a contrast! Both are beautiful in their own way, one sort of picture postcard, the other sculptured like a wild work of art. Each is shaped, as men are, by the conditions around it.

There is a Safeway grocery store, right outside the road to the archery range, that has a good delicatessen. If you want to picnic on the beach, you may buy sandwich makings there.

4

Ocean Beach and the Cliff House

Driving: Go straight out Geary Street to the end of it (it changes names from Geary Street to Geary Boulevard to Point Lobos Avenue, but it's the same street and you can't get lost).

Public Transportation: The No. 2 Clement bus, caught on Sutter Street two blocks up from Union Square, will take you within a block and a half of the Cliff House.

The No. 38 Geary, caught on Geary Street, and the No. 2 McAllister, caught on Market Street will both take you to Ocean Beach below the Cliff House.

This area offers a remarkable combination of long, sandy beaches; heavy surf pounding against high rocks; and wild ocean animals, close at hand, not found anywhere else in the world—certainly not within the limits of a major city.

Ocean Beach

By a wonderful combination of luck, nature, and foresight, the whole of OCEAN BEACH, from the Cliff House almost to the county line, is public park land. This means complete public access to almost six miles of level sandy beach on the western edge of our city.

Ocean Beach would be the Riviera of the West Coast except for the weather and the water.

The water of the Japanese Current flowing down from the north is always around 55 degrees, summer and winter. The coldness of the water would preclude swimming by any but the hardiest even if it weren't for the dangerous undertow and rip tides found along Ocean Beach. The beach is posted against swimming, and one should heed the warning. Especially watch the littler kids when they wade along the edge. The slope of the beach makes the receding waves suck the sand from under their feet, causing them to lose their footing. The cold water means that there is usually a cold wind, or if not cold, brisk. It also means fog along the coast mornings and evenings during the summer.

These are the negative aspects of Ocean Beach. The positive aspects are almost without number. Ocean Beach is a wonderful place to stroll; to build sand castles; to surf fish; to beachcomb; to watch the myriad forms of bird life and sea life; to run; to thrill at close hand to the kind of crashing breakers shown in every oil seascape ever painted; to get your feet wet when a wave you didn't see sneaked up on you and caught you; and, after your shoes are already soaked, to stand in a receding wave and feel it tug the sand from under your feet and to wonder at the power of the sea, felt on a small scale through the sand under your shoes.

Low tide is the best time to find wave-smoothed, beautiful rocks and shells not yet pounded to pieces. In Chapter 19, you'll find instructions on how to read a tide table. (Tide tables are found in the weather section of the daily newspapers.) On Ocean Beach, opposite the Zoo, you can find whole sand dollars at low tide. The pretty rocks you will pick up all along the beach are sometimes of semiprecious nature— agate and jasper—that will polish well in your home rock tumblers. Small pieces of sand- and wave-smoothed driftwood are to be found everywhere and make a nice souvenir of San Francisco that you can use as a setting for your potted plants at home. It's a good idea to take along a paper bag from the grocery store because your kids will keep bringing you stuff that they want to keep and you'll end up with sandy pockets otherwise. The variety of dead sea animals and plants washed up on the beach is enormous, ranging from tiny crabs to dead sea lions, from jellyfish to bull-whiplike kelp fronds twenty feet long. There is also an enormous amount of garbage washed up on the beach out of the ocean. Those plastic jugs and bottles and junk weren't thrown away from San Francisco; it's from more northerly and southerly cities that use the ocean for a garbage dump, and from the ships at sea. If you bring any paper or cans to Ocean Beach, be sure to take them with you when you leave.

If there's a word for Ocean Beach, it must be "exhilarating." You get so involved in the crashing surf, the sand, the wind, the birds and found things that after any visit, there's a letdown when you leave. You know you've been somewhere and will carry away good memories.

Cliff House Area

Abruptly rising from the sand of Ocean Beach is the steep ring of rocky heights that forms the entrance to the Golden Gate (the opening into San Francisco Bay). Where the sand of Ocean Beach runs into the Cliff House cliffs, you can see excellent examples of the toughness of sea life in the barnacles that thrive on the wave-pounded rocks. The change is immediate and dramatic—from dead sea level to the complex of shops and restaurants two-hundred feet above. There are three places to visit here (and an unlawful fourth).

The first is the CLIFF HOUSE area itself. If you haven't picnicked on the beach, there are restaurants for sit-down meals, as well as coffee shops for snacks and take-out food and drink. As at any major attraction, there are souvenir shops for momentos, and some interesting features, such as a "penny arcade" with mechanical games and music machines. Most of these machines are antique pieces salvaged from the old Sutro Baths collection (a small portion; collectors have the rest). One work of painstaking perfection is a whole carnival made of toothpicks.

The broad, several-leveled viewing areas behind the Cliff House give excellent views of the crashing surf, the ocean, and especially SEAL and BIRD ROCKS. Almost all year around, you may see "seals" on Seal Rock; all year around, you'll find large sea birds on Bird Rock a short distance away. The "seals" are really Steller sea lions—the kind you see in the circuses. Seals are more ancient in their adaptation to the sea, lack external ears, and have tiny front flippers. At the Bio–Sonar Laboratories at Coyote Hills Regional Park (see page 000) you can examine these sea mammals more closely. Seals look rather like big sausages and hump themselves along the ground in quick, bouncing movements. The sea lions you see on Seal Rock are more recently adapted to the sea and their front flippers can be used as legs—or to applaud with in the circus shows. No bouncing here; indeed, they are mountain climbers. Look at the sheer slopes of Seal Rock either through your binoculars or through the dime-in-the-slot telescopes available on the view pavilion of the Cliff House and you'll see what I mean. The rock is dead steep and they have to fling themselves on it on a high wave; then they begin to climb. Often, you see them thirty or forty feet up on the rocky ledges of Seal Rock, hronking and basking in the sun. Now, it may be easy for such a beast to pull itself *up* a steep, rocky island, but their hind legs are only flippers. To this day, I don't know how in the world they get down.

The fascinating thing is that these are wild sea beasts, as wild as grizzly bears, mountain sheep, or timber wolves, coyotes or free-ranging buffalo. That they congregate on these rocks a stone's throw from one of the world's most densely populated cities is a continuing miracle. Of course, by local and ancient legislation, the sea lions are official citizens of San Francisco, enjoying all the rights and privileges. It's a vote of confidence for the city that they have continued to come here and not move to the suburbs. Bird Rock is also full of exotic flying beasts—cormorants, albatross, gulls, terns, and an occasional brown pelican.

Opposite the Cliff House, toward the city, you'll see a curious cliff. It looks strange, and it should. At first glance, you think it's natural rock, but then you realize that natural rock doesn't look *exactly* that way. It's all textured concrete, designed to keep the crumbly natural cliff from falling down onto the road. On top of that cliff are the beautifully landscaped grounds that surrounded ADOLPH SUTRO'S MANSION. It's a city park, the mansion having long burned down. To reach it, walk up the street leading to the Cliff House and turn right just past the parking lot.

Adolph Sutro was a civil engineer who made millions from the most impressive engineering feat of his day, drilling an impossible tunnel through the mountains of Nevada to drain water from the silver diggings of the Comstock Lode. As you can tell from the ruins and the grounds, the mansion must have been magnificent. The view from what was the west portico is one of the very finest in San Francisco. It surveys the whole sweep of Ocean Beach, Golden Gate Park, and the western edge of the city. Here is an unsurpassed view of the ocean to the FARALLON ISLANDS nearly thirty miles to the west (if the weather is clear). San

Francisco is a tiny city in land area (only about seven miles to the side, roughly forty-five square miles—it's smaller than Dayton, Ohio), but it controls a vast, watery empire. The Farallon Islands are legally part of San Francisco.

Across the street from Sutro Park is a road labeled EL CAMINO DEL MAR. This road used to lead around the edge of the city to Lincoln Park and thence to the Presidio. It is closed at this point and again just below the Legion of Honor museum in Lincoln Park because of landslides. This spot offers an excellent view of the Golden Gate, the mile-wide entrance to San Francisco Bay. It's a wonderful place for photographs of ships entering and leaving the Bay. There is also a fine monument here, the command bridge of the cruiser U. S. S. *San Francisco.* This ship played an important role in the battle of Leyte Gulf in the sea war with Japan during World War II. The account of its accomplishments on the monument is fascinating reading. The command bridge is a graphic example of the horrors of warfare—riddled with direct hits, that punched holes through the steel armor, then exploded at leg level. It takes a brave man to put himself in such a position of danger, and many men died here. Let's hope that this is as close to war as kids will ever get; but let them see this so they won't think war is what they imagine or what they see on the television.

When you look down from the Cliff House of the U. S. S. *San Francisco,* you'll see people walking down below and fishing from the rocks into the crashing surf. You wonder how they got there and how you can get there too. I hesitate to tell you, because it's posted property and I'm not one to lead visitors to our fair city into any wrongdoing, no matter how modestly illegal the act is. The following is only to satisfy your curiosity and never in the world to suggest that you should go down there to walk around the foundations of the old Sutro Baths or through the tunnels or out onto the rock, where others are catching three-foot-long sea bass. From Merrie Way, one road down from El Camino del Mar, there are gaping holes under the chain-link fence through which I have witnessed countless trespassers walk (these are *big* holes) down the hill. There is an interesting series of paths that lead around the hill from the U. S. S. *San Francisco,* and I have noticed that several end in holes in the fence and thus lead down onto the rock. Thank goodness I have never been tempted to bend the law and follow those many unembarrassed illegal entrants, many with kids, to look at this very interesting part of the Cliff House area.

The Ocean Beach–Cliff House area is a major point on your visit to San Francisco, for grand views of the ocean and the Golden Gate, for extraordinary wild sea beasts almost at your fingertips, and for a good, close look at the ocean. But watch the time if you're on a schedule. You go to the Cliff House just to look at the sea lions and discover that the *surf is up* (even with the cold water and the undertow, Ocean Beach is one of the best surfing areas on the West Coast—the enthusiasts wear wet suits). As they paddle out into the waves, you see little black flecks that are the surfers' heads (you can tell the little black flecks that are the surfers' heads from the little black flecks that are the heads of the hunting sea lions very easily—the surfers are the ones pushing surf boards). The surfers paddle beyond Seal Rocks, turn around and paddle like mad to catch a wave, then very gracefully rise to their feet. Nine times out of ten, they fall off immediately and have to swim like mad to rescue their surf boards. When one manages to catch a wave and ride it in, you understand why the sport is so popular. But there are many little things like this that can detain you, so allow for them.

5

Views

SAN FRANCISCO IS FAMOUS for its views. It's a hilly city
and these hills look out upon glorious things. To an
adult, a view is an aesthetic experience. Kids, on the
other hand, especially preteen kids, don't quite look
upon a view as an aesthetic experience; and for an
adult to drive and drive just to get to a view is merely another aspect of adult madness. To younger kids,
a view is a fact—younger kids are narrowly logical.
Adults drive up a hill, stop, and exclaim, "Isn't that
a wonderful view!" Younger kids think, "Well, of
course it is! When you get high up on a hill, there's
bound to be a view—and what's the big deal?" There
are only three kinds of view the smaller kids find
glorious: if you can climb on it, it's great; if there is
imminent danger that you can fall off it, it's even
better; and if it can be tied into something *else* that
is interesting or exciting, the view is worth while (like
the three views around the Cliff House, burned mansion, sea lions, battleship—all of them with things to
climb on and fall off).

Most of the natural views in San Francisco conform
to these criteria. The most popular tourist views will
be listed first, then some glorious views that are not
only suitable for little kids, but are special for adults
as well and enough off the beaten path to give the

whole family something extra to remember about your visit to San Francisco.

Twin Peaks

The view from TWIN PEAKS is the most famous view in San Francisco. Unfortunately, there's no public transportation to it, so it must be done by car (or sightseeing bus). The easiest way from Union Square is to drive one block up Geary Street to Mason street and turn left (both are one way in the right direction) down to Market Street and then turn right. Stay on Market all the way out to the base of Twin Peaks (where Market Street suddenly becomes Portola Drive). At this writing and for several years to come, there will be detours as the construction for BART is completed, but just follow the Market Street signs. Follow the boulevard around the curve of the hill. When you crest the hill, get in the right lane. In a few blocks you'll come to Twin Peaks Boulevard and turn right. The road leads up to Twin Peaks and forms a figure eight around the top of the peaks, so you are able to take in the whole panorama of the city. Park at the radio-transmitting towers in the parking area—there are usually several sightseeing buses there, so you can't miss it.

The views from Twin Peaks are very grand and it's a fine place for photographs. The views from the parking area look generally east and north. Let me describe briefly what you are seeing when you look from this view. The long suspension-cantilever bridge is the BAY BRIDGE. It's easy to keep the Bay Bridge and the Golden Gate Bridge separate. The Bay Bridge has X-shaped trusses in the towers, while the Golden Gate Bridge's towers are square trussed: the Bay Bridge is silver, the Golden Gate Bridge is orange. The two sections of the Bay Bridge are anchored at

Yerba Buena Island; the long spit of land to the left of Yerba Buena is Treasure Island. It was formed on the shallows with fill dredged during the construction of the Bay Bridge. Treasure Island was the site of the 1939 Golden Gate Exposition that was held to celebrate the completion of the two bridges across the Bay. It was to become a seaport for the famous China Clippers—the passenger sea planes that flew between here and points west. At the outbreak of World War II, Treasure Island became a naval base and so it remains today.

The bridge leads to Oakland. To the left of the bridge, just before the hills, you may see a tall, slender structure—the bell tower on the campus of the University of California at Berkeley. In San Francisco, most of the area to the right of the bridge is the Mission District. The broad street that comes more or less straight toward you is Market Street. Alcatraz is the low, rocky island closest to us to the left of Treasure Island. There are plans to open it to tourists in the summer of 1974. Beyond Alcatraz, the other, larger island in the Bay is Angel Island. Downtown is more or less pinpointed by the huge, oil-colored building that is the headquarters of the Bank of America. The twin-spired church in town around to your left is Saint Ignatius; the domed structure farther out is the Temple Emanu-El. The wide strip of green running off to your left is Golden Gate Park, and the triangle of green in the city far-view is the Presidio of San Francisco, the headquarters of the Sixth Army.

The point on which you are standing is almost exactly twice as high above sea level as Chicago. Also, this particular area of California was extremely heavily populated by Indians in the olden days. In fact, what with the abundance of sea life, game animals on land, and edible plants, California supported more Indians than any other area in America. These peaks were venerated by the local Indians and it is extremely possible that you will be able to find "Indian stones" in the very parking lot where you stand. (The red chert with which the area is graveled breaks naturally into what looks almost like arrowheads, hand axes, and spear points. It's not entirely a lie. The stones that you look at on Twin Peaks were looked at by the local Indians a millenium before the Spanish came.)

Coit Tower

The second most famous San Francisco view is that from COIT TOWER atop TELEGRAPH HILL. You can reach it, driving from Union Square, by following the Powell Street cable-car tracks up Powell, turning left when they do up one block to Mason Street, then following Mason down the hill to Lombard Street. Then turn right. Drive up Lombard to the crest, following the signs. If you prefer to forget the car, walk two blocks up to Sutter and Stockton and take the Stockton Street bus through the tunnel. Get off at Union Street and take the Coit Tower bus that stops at Union and Columbus (Washington Square, where the big church is). It's not a terribly long walk through the tunnel along Stockton to Union Street and you will be walking through the fringes of Chinatown and into the heart of Italian North Beach. Once you get through the tunnel, Grant Avenue is one block down to your right, so you can walk through Chinatown itself if you like, cross Broadway, and keep on Columbus Avenue to Union Street.

Coit Tower and Telegraph Hill offer a spectacular view of the North Bay and the waterfront: both the hill and the tower are rather special San Francisco things. In the days when San Francisco was linked to the rest of the world only by sail and steamships, there was a "telegraph" on top of this hill. It was a two-armed semaphore on a tower that signaled to the city the arrival of ships passing through the Golden Gate. The position of the arms (as when Boy Scouts or sailors signal with two flags) would indicate the kind of ship that had arrived. This was the "telegraph" for which the hill was named. The long pole with the ball, on the hill now, is a replica of another feature of the hill. It was a service of the Port. An official would raise the ball, and, precisely at noon, would let it fall, so the ships in the Bay could set their chronometers to the right time. (The correct time was necessary for navigation purposes before there were such things as radio beacons.)

Coit Tower was given to the city by Lilly Hitchcock Coit, a wealthy San Francisco eccentric. She was a fire buff from the days of the volunteer fire brigades. That was strictly a manly avocation, but she was "adopted" by the No. 5 Knickerbocker Company and to the end of her days wore a piece of jewelry with a 5 in the design. She donated the sculpture of the firemen in Washington Square down the hill and this tower, which is supposed to be a stylized fire hose nozzel.

There are various-leveled pavements to run on and jump from. The dime-in-the-slot telescopes give you a close look at Alcatraz, the bridges, sailboats on the Bay, and the waterfront. There is a wider view from the top of the tower, which means a two-hundred-foot elevator ride (modest charge), which is fun. The ground-floor interior of the tower is decorated with some very interesting murals completed in the 1930s. For the last several years they have been under restoration (and probably will be for some years to come) because of damage done by vandals, so you can't get a close look at them. Walk around and look in the windows, though. The people are in the costumes of the 1930s and one panel is especially interesting. You'll see a San Francisco street scene with radical newspapers (*The Worker, The New Masses*); a hold-up in broad daylight; a movie advertising

Charlie Chaplin's *City Lights*—all of which go to show that though times are different, people haven't changed much. The little kids can play on the railings outside while the older kids look through the windows.

Golden Gate Bridge

There are three wonderful views on and around the GOLDEN GATE BRIDGE, which will probably be one of the high points of your visit. There's no direct public transportation, so go by car or tour bus.

To get to the bridge from Union Square, go out Geary Street to Van Ness Avenue (the first large boulevard—about eight blocks) and turn right. Stay in the left lane and follow the Highway 101 and Golden Gate Bridge signs. You'll turn left onto Lombard Street, which will take you to the approach to the bridge. After you pass the Presidio, get in the right lane. As you approach the toll plaza, you'll see a sign directing you to the view area and the Presidio. Turn right at the first opportunity before you get to the toll plaza, or you'll have to go across the bridge. If you miss the turn-off, cross the bridge and go into the view area on the other side. (It's going to cost you 75¢ to get back so you might as well enjoy the magnificent city view from the Marin anchorage.) When you leave there, keep in the right lane again and take the first right and follow the signs that direct you back to San Francisco. Again, keep in the right lane and head for the toll gate on the extreme right. After you pay your toll, take the first right around and under the toll plaza and you're where you should have been in the first place. I've included this because what with the press of traffic and your first visit there, it's not hard to miss it. Don't feel like a dummy if you do—first-time native visitors do the same thing. The view from under the toll plaza is fine for several reasons. The view is excellent—a wonderful place for photographs. There is ample parking here. You can examine the complicated girder understructure of the bridge from this point. Also, near the statue of Mr. Joseph B. Strauss, the engineer who designed the bridge, is a section of one of the cables that holds up the bridge. With all the steel beneath, it's easy to forget that the whole thing is held up by two yard-thick cables (27,520 quarter-inch steel wires making up a cable) that pass over the towers and are anchored in immense blocks of concrete at either end. The girder understructure gives no support whatsoever, merely stiffens the sixty-foot-wide roadbed (with ten-foot sidewalks on either side). Here is a quick description of how this suspension bridge was built.

As the roadway approaches were started from either side, the foundations of the towers were excavated. This meant sinking caissons down to bedrock beneath the water, an enormously complicated job in this area of extremely strong tides. The towers were built to the height of about 750 feet (the roadbed is about 250 feet above the water), and small wire cables were towed across by boat, then lifted to the tops of the towers. These small wire ropes drew heavier lines until a trackway for the cable stringers was formed so they could begin the actual work of drawing over the wire strands that would eventually become the cable. A cable stringer went back and forth along the cable line, playing out strands of wire —and back and forth twenty-four hours a day. (The bridge took four years to build.) When enough wire was laid, another machine was sent up that compressed the wires and wrapped them so that the cable was round. Where the wires come down to the anchorage, they separate from the yard-thick cable to several smaller parts, then to even smaller sections, and finally to almost individual strands in a three-dimensional fan, locked into the concrete with a myriad of lead and steel collars.

The bridge moves, as can be seen in the two expansion joints you'll bounce over as you drive across it. (They look like sideways steel gates.) The bridge expands and contracts with the heat. This means that the cables also move, and, atop the towers, you won't find the cables just sitting there, but riding on rollers. The suspension cables that come down from the main cable and attach to the steel girders supporting the roadbed are called "suspenders."

A suspension bridge is a very complicated apparatus and the section of cable in the view area explains much about how it's built. When you look at the individual strands of wire in the cable section, you wonder how they can hold up the immense weight of the steel girders, the six-lane concrete highway, and the cars on the roadbed that are crossing bumper to bumper during the rush hour. There are eighty thousand miles of these quarter-inch wires to do the work and when you consider that three strands of this wire could lift up a car easily, you begin to understand the immense strength of the cables.

As I say, there are three great views from the bridge. The first is from the view area below the toll plaza. The second is from the deck of the bridge itself. As I said, the roadbed is about 250 feet above the water—a height that permits an unparalled view of the city, the Bay, the East Bay, the Bay Islands, sailboats, freighters passing beneath you, or, if you're extremely lucky, the turbulence of one of our nuclear submarines sneaking out. The channel beneath the bridge is in excess of three hundred feet deep, and they leave San Francisco Bay submerged when they have a mind to, but the wake shows because they're huge ships. There is a great walk from the parking area beneath the toll plaza to the second tower and back again. Warning: this is a real walk because the suspension part of the bridge is almost a mile wide, and if you have smaller kids, you have to take that into consideration.

There are other things to take into consideration when you walk the bridge. As I mentioned before, the Golden Gate is the only sea-level opening to the interior valley, and that means, in summer, that the wind is whistling right through here and it's cold. Usually, it's also foggy in unusual ways. When you walk the bridge deck, sometimes you can't see the tops of the towers because of the fog, or the bridge is in bright sunlight and you can't see the water beneath. These are real wonders to those who have never seen real fog, and it's thrilling to those who have lived here all their lives. It's a good idea to take along sweaters any time of the year when you walk the bridge.

Another thing is the danger of the bridge, real and imagined. I am frightened of heights. People do things on the bridge that make me cringe, such as lifting their little children to the railing for a better look (it's 250 feet down!). To fellow acrophobes, let me assure you that it's probably the safest bridge for walking in the world. The railings are as high as a man's chest, and the pickets are so close together that even a two-year-old couldn't squeeze through. The sheer height may make you uncomfortable, but it is certified safe.

The third Golden Gate Bridge view is across the road in the PRESIDIO. Drive over from the Golden Gate Bridge view area through the tunnel beneath the highway and turn right immediately on the first road —don't go back onto the highway. Pull off and park on the rough gravel road near the low concrete structure you see on your right. It's one of the coastal gun emplacements built during World War II to protect the Golden Gate. There are tunnellike powder magazines beneath and the foundations for shore batteries above. (The guns have long since been replaced by guided missile sites in the Presidio.) Here there are great things to climb on and an unsurpassed view of the entrance to the Golden Gate—again, a great place for photos. This view has the added advantage that it is relatively unknown, both to tourists and natives, even though it's only a hundred yards away from the bridge.

If, as a tourist with children, you see the views from the Cliff House, Twin Peaks, Coit Tower, and the Golden Gate Bridge, you may rest assured that you have covered the major bases as far as views go in San Francisco. This list, of course, leaves out the views from buildings (such as restaurants, hotels, and bars). The views are usually not exciting to kids anyway, and the buildings usually don't go out of their way to welcome little ones.

There are more neat views in San Francisco that will be mentioned in connection with their related points of interest, such as the wonderful view from CORONA HEIGHTS, where the JOSEPHINE D. RANDALL JUNIOR MUSEUM is located. The nice thing about San Francisco is that, in this hilly city, you go somewhere to see something special, and the nature of the city gives you something extra for free.

6

The Embarcadero

FROM its earliest days, San Francisco has been a major port—and an exotic one. It's one of the chief centers of trade with the Far East and a processing center for coffee, spices, and food products (as well as a clearing house for manufactured products). Even the quickest ride along our port street, THE EMBARCADERO, is an exciting experience. If you've never seen a major port at work, you're in for a grand adventure.

A few notes before we begin. Our port is divided by the Ferry Building into two parts. The piers to the south are even-numbered, while the piers to the north are odd-numbered. The piers to the south generally handle freight, while the piers to the north handle both freight and passenger liners. Since all the piers are on the east side of the street, the best way to see the most is to drive out to the end of the interesting part (where you can get closest to the ships) and come back on the right side of the street. The traffic is too dangerous to try to cross the street to the piers. When you look at the ships, remember that you're looking at an enormously complicated three-dimensional jigsaw puzzle. Freighters are merely floating warehouses. Bits and pieces of cargo are packed in and unloaded at every port of call. It's quite a problem to stow the cargo for San Francisco so that the cargo headed for Vancouver doesn't have to be

shifted before the San Francisco cargo can be unloaded. The problem is complicated by the high cost
of dockside labor, such as longshoremen. To operate
efficiently, both the fore and aft cargo hatches should
be worked at the same time. It takes considerable skill
to accomplish this, and the chief officer, who handles
the stowing, is highly trained indeed.

I've used the expression "the Embarcadero" to
cover the whole of our waterfront port facilities, even
though the street called The Embarcadero runs only
from near Fisherman's Wharf to Pier 46.

The best way to see the port is to drive down
Stockton Street at Union Square and cross over Market Street onto Fourth Street. It's one way out. Turn
left at Townsend Street, when you reach the Southern
Pacific Railroad tracks, then turn right on Third
Street. Almost immediately, you'll cross over one of
the two drawbridges in town. This is a cantilevered
bridge, and, if you're lucky, you'll be able to watch it
operate either on your way out or on your way back.
Drive out Third Street, keeping in the left-hand lane,
and turn left on Twentieth Street. Turn left again on
Illinois Street (the flashing yellow light), and you'll
begin to get the feel of ships and the port. The buildings to your right are the Bethlehem Steel shipyards.
There's nothing little about ocean-going ships and
you'll see the huge pieces of steel and gigantic bits of
machinery that go into building and refitting ships.
Around here there are also yards that work on sports
fishing craft. Keep to your right where Illinois joins
China Basin Street. You'll see MISSION ROCK RESORT
and its sign, "Beer Bait Boats." This is a fisherman's
hangout, a restaurant–bar–rowboat-rental place with
a deck over the Bay. Here, with a pair of binoculars,
you can watch the ship-refitting at the Bethlehem
yards to your right and the work going on at the
Triple-A Machine Shops to your left. Bethlehem seems
to handle mostly civilian freighter and ocean-liner
work. Triple-A handles this, and also refits military

ships, Coast Guard and Navy. It's a great spot to watch those huge ships' cranes do their work and marvel at the problems of keeping something as big as a floating ten-story building (lying on its side) in good repair. Mission Rock Resort has soft drinks and sandwiches, beer and coffee. If you're interested, you can rent rowboats to try your luck with the rock cod and sea bass that seem to abound here.

Continue down China Basin Street to Pier 54. This is one of the two piers that handles cross-Bay railroad barges. If you're lucky, you'll catch them when freight cars are being loaded or unloaded on the barges. Be sure to stop and watch; it's one of the few places where this activity can be seen anywhere.

Piers 48A and 48B are good places to get a close look at the working of the ships. After leaving Pier 48, you'll recross the drawbridge on Third Street. Take the first right at Berry Street and continue. You can usually get a good look at the ships at Piers 32 and 30, and, in this vicinity, you will also be able to examine the steel bracing for the roadway of the Bay Bridge.

Just before you get to the Ferry Building, you'll pass the AGRICULTURE BUILDING, which might seem a strange thing to find on the waterfront. Truth is, California and the Federal Agriculture Agency spend huge amounts of money in San Francisco; more, indeed, than in some of the agricultural counties around us. This large outlay goes into inspection of imports. Frozen Australian beef, New Zealand lamb, canned Japanese shrimp, Formosan mushrooms, Philippine dried and frozen fish are sampled and tested here for wholesomeness. Coffee, tea, cocoa, spices, copra, jute, wood products, bamboo packaging, mahogany veneer —in a word, everything that comes in that might harbor bad bugs or plant disease, or items improperly labeled, is examined by an army of inspectors. Though not obvious, it is an extremely important function of the port officials.

The Ferry Building

Now to the FERRY BUILDING and the wonders in and around it. It's a nice break to park here and take in some of the cultural aspects of the Embarcadero. The Ferry Building itself is an interesting place. This was the main terminal for the ferry boats that served the Bay before the bridges were built. Inside are two things worth seeing.

WORLD TRADE CENTER. This is to the left of the entrance and holds the offices for many of the official trading groups that do business with San Francisco. There are displays of national products, grand murals showing the wealth of peoples, and products of the Far East and South Seas. It's interesting to walk through.

CALIFORNIA GEOLOGY MUSEUM. This is up the stairs of the main entrance and to your right. The hours are 8 AM–5 PM, Monday–Friday; 10 AM–noon, the first Saturday of every month; and it's free.

Maintained by the California Division of Mines and Geology, this museum-library is a fascinating place for the rockhound and layman alike. So much wealth in California comes from its mineral resources that a lot of care has gone into making this museum interesting. The first things you see are elegant collections of huge specimens of mineral crystals; precious and semiprecious gem stones gathered in California and elsewhere; and six-inch-thick steel bank vaults crammed with gold dust, gold nuggets, and gold quartz. In the main room to your left are cases showing representative mineral samples from each county in California. Along one wall here are collectors' specimens of mineral crystals of every description. The other walls hold displays of finished products manufactured from the raw minerals. Many of the displays also show the processing procedure. At the main desk, one may buy all kinds of maps, books, and booklets (and, as is usual in a government printing, at bargain rates). You may be interested in the books and booklets on California earthquakes: where they happen, why, and how to be safe in an earthquake. They also have a "Gold Pack"—a collection of pamphlets showing where you're likely to find gold and how to pan for gold and build sluices, long toms, rockers, and so forth. There are state geologists on duty here, and if you bring in a rock, they are usually able to identify it for you. That's how we found out that a pretty, multicolored rock we picked up near Napa was an opal—common opal, but still opal. Although this museum is not usually thought of as one of the city's major museums, it is one of the major geology museums of the state and worth a special visit.

Vaillancourt Fountain, Hyatt Regency Hotel, and Embarcadero Park

All these features are brand-new to San Francisco and they're great! Space to build them came from a massive redevelopment clearance on the north side of the Ferry Building. When I first came here in 1958, this area was full of slum hotels, deadfall bars, and sleazy shops to serve the merchant seamen and longshoremen. A little to the north was San Francisco's Wholesale Produce area—noted for being crowded and congested, with rats as big as cats. It has all been cleaned out, new buildings built, and open spaces made available that were never even there before in the history of the city. Literally! The original shoreline along this stretch was around Montgomery Street. All this new area is filled Bay land, and as soon as the shallows were filled, they were built upon. It was (and is) valuable land. The Bay now comes to the Embarcadero. One of the reasons that freight-

ers and ocean liners can dock so near the street is
that they're docking in water that used to be a good
fifteen-minute row out in the Bay from the original
shoreline. During the excavation of the BART tunnel
up Market Street from the Ferry Building, the diggers
cut their way through old ships abandoned by the
gold-seekers of 1849 and the piers of old wharves
covered by the fill.

EMBARCADERO PLAZA and VAILLAINCOURT FOUN-
TAIN. This huge, open space at the foot of Market
Street is a great picnic spot. In the Ferry Building
there is a quick lunch place where you can get take-out
sandwiches, and on the side streets around the plaza
are snack bars that cater to office workers. Here a
picnic can be organized. Running space, a fountain,
the street vendors . . . you can rest or frolic here to
your heart's content. The plaza is one of several designated spots in San Francisco where craftsmen and
-women can sell their stuff. There are fine selections
of small crafts, belts, macramé, jewelry, art, weaving,
carvings, and the like, that are sold by the people
who made them. Since the wares are small, the artists
usually work between sales and you can see how they
do it. It's a wonderful experience for kids who have
never seen anything made, and who believe, just like
the aboriginal Cargo Cultists of New Guinea, that
made things are created magically by the stores that
sell them. The street fairs and art fairs listed in the
calendar in this book should be taken in just for this
education. Kids, of course, believe they can do anything once they see an expert do it. Watching these
people work on leather, or metal, or whatever gives
them unbounded confidence that they can do as well.
I know that every visit there starts some grand project in my little boy, and we all get involved and learn
a lot.

The Vaillaincourt Fountain in the Plaza is the most
maligned work of art in the city, both as a sculpture
and as a fountain. God knows, at first glance, it is a

funny-looking jumble of concrete. Square conduits go off in all directions; water spouts, pours and splashes from crude squares, like the emptying of a myriad of angular hip boots; one sees steam hissing out from several points. From everyone who has ever seen a fountain, the first reaction is that if that is a fountain, I am a leaping butterfly! The whole thing is absurd. But then again, it's one of the few fountains in the world that invites you to walk on, in, over, and through it, getting nearly splashed at every turn and hissed at with steam, with its own feeling of danger and mystery. The local critics who have deplored the expense of the thing and say it has bruised their artistic sensibilities are like the rest of us who just look at the thing and say it's crazy. Kids usually have a good feeling of what's good and what's phony and bad . . . and if you follow them along the square stepping stones an inch above the pool, walk under the square conduits spewing water on every side, lean against the railing looking down on the thing from above, you'll find that it's probably the best fountain you've every experienced.

HYATT REGENCY HOTEL. Just off the plaza is one of the most wonderful buildings in town, the Hyatt Regency Hotel. The whole thing is absurdly spectacular. From the outside, you can't quite make out why the building slopes. That's what I said, the building slopes in a grand staircase of balconies. Once inside, you understand. The lobby seems like one of the highest enclosed spaces in the world. It has to be seen to be believed. The sloping balconies of the rooms form the ceiling of the lobby; tent-roofed, lighted elevators, like half carousels, slide up and down the wall opposite the slanted ceiling; a huge sculpture, as big as a small house—a kind of modified geodesic dome— looks little in the middle of the immense space; good-sized trees, with caged white doves, line sunken eating areas: it is both a place and a fantasy.

SAUSALITO FERRY. Just to the north of the Ferry

Building is the small ferry terminal. I've described
the great bargain our ferry rides are in Chapter 2.
For all the events in and around the Ferry Building you can find public parking at Pier 1 and 7.

North of the Ferry Building

Continuing along The Embarcadero you can get
good shots of the freighters being unloaded at several
points, and you'll see some special things. Pier 7 is
a public fishing pier (rebuilt after it burned down in
1973), and there are other fishing spots on the loading
and cargo areas between the piers on this section of
The Embarcadero. On the public piers, no fishing
license is required; but there are limits as to catch or
size of fish. (See page 145.) Pier 35 is an especially
interesting pier, in that it handles the bulk of the
ocean-passenger-liner dockage. Stop if there is an
ocean liner in port (in the summer, the liner trade is
especially active). They are something to see—glorious things. The liners are floating hotels seven to ten
stories high and as long as a football field or longer.
There are sleek, rather petite liners like the *Spirit of
London* and monsters like the *Monterey* or the *Ham-
burg* that regularly stop here. If you're lucky, you'll be
here when the *Canberra* docks. Like the Hyatt Regency, it is outrageously spectacular. It looks as if it
was designed by a 1930s Hollywood musical extrava-
ganza director, but the thing's real. Just go to the visitors' section (the guard at the gate will direct you)
and you'll get a good shot at the ship. Try to be there
when it sails and you'll be able to hear the band and
watch the streamers being thrown from shipdeck—
just as in the movies.

Piers 37, 41, and sometimes 43 are of interest because the visiting foreign warships usually tie up to
these piers. They're usually training cruises of naval-
academy midshipmen—and good will, diplomatic

visits, trade fair events. Last year, there were French, German, English, and Japanese training ships in port during the summer. In each case, there was an opportunity to tour the ships, talk to the sailors, and get nice souvenirs of the visit. The arrivals are especially nice to catch. The Navy Band is there, as are local dignitaries, foreign consuls, and welcome committees, as well as radio and TV reporters. It's a big show and good to take in if you have the chance. The local newspapers announce the events, so check the papers (the shipping section that's usually on the weather page) to see where the freighters and ocean liners can be seen.

7

Shopping with Kids in San Francisco

There is nothing quite so frustrating than to be surrounded by fascinating shops for adults and have to forgo your pleasure because the children are bored. The following is a short list of very special shopping areas and places nearby that kids love. Surprisingly, they are generally close to each other, so that each parent can take an hour to shop in peace while the other takes care of the kids. Be assured that these aren't the only shopping areas in San Francisco—there are fine and unusual shops all through the city—but not geared to the enjoyment of the whole family, as are the areas listed here.

Downtown

One of the finest shopping areas in the city is a rough triangle bounded by Powell Streets, Post and Sutter Streets (with the emphasis on Post), and Market Street. Within this relatively small area one may find huge department stores, such as Macy's and the Emporium; elegant men's and women's specialty shops, great gift stores such as Gump's—all kinds of strictly big-city furniture, jewelry, art galleries, boutiques, indeed, nearly anything you can think of. Since this area is smack in the middle of downtown, you might not think there are places that kids would like, but there's even a playground for toddlers nearby— and we'll start with that.

HUNTINGTON PARK. Nob Hill; California Street between Mason and Taylor Streets. Near the Mark Hopkins and Fairmont Hotels.

Take the cable car (either one) to California and transfer to the California Street car going up the hill. Get off at Mason and California and enter the park in the middle of the block.

This is a tony playground indeed in that it is located on some of the most expensive real estate in the world, the grounds of what was once the Huntington mansion—burned in the earthquake-fire. The large brownstone mansion on the corner was originally owned by the Flood family. Now it's the Pacific Union Club, an association of millionaires. The park is where the two fountains are. You'll see swings, slides, and sandboxes on the side away from California Street. If you take a ball to toss around, this is suitable for younger kids—from one to five.

F. A. O. SCHWARZ TOYS. 180 Post Street (at Post Street and Grant Avenue). It's not at all hard to spend an hour here with the kids. Be prepared to buy something—because the goods are so enticing, you certainly will. For all ages. (See page 228.)

BANK OF CALIFORNIA MUSEUM. 400 California Street (at California and Sansome Streets). Go down Post to Montgomery, left to California, and right a block to Sansome. Gold coins, bullion, and currencies. For children six and older. (See Chapter 10.)

WELLS FARGO HISTORY ROOM. 420 Montgomery Street. Go down Post to Montgomery; turn left to 420. Exciting Gold Rush exhibits and gold. For children four and older. (See Chapter 10.)

CABLE-CAR BARN AND MUSEUM. Washington and Mason Streets. Take the Powell Street cable car and get off at Washington. For children four and up. (See Chapter 10.)

CHINATOWN. Chinatown is nearby. It's best to visit with the whole family, but if you've been there, the kids won't mind going again. Go down Post to Grant, then up Grant. (See Chapter 11.)

THE EMPORIUM. 835 Market Street. This is the largest store in town. If Mamma wants to check the basement for bargains (good buys in kids' clothing and shoes), Dad can take the little ones to the good toy department or the older ones to the hobby, coin, or book departments.

Food and Bathrooms Downtown.

Every parent knows that kids never have to go when they are leaving their hotel or motel room or get hungry when they are passing a restaurant. (This is one eternal truth in this world of shades of gray). No, kids *always* have to go—and right now!—when you are in the middle of the downtown of a strange city. Same thing when they are dying of starvation! No need to fret about the bathroom problem. (Women seem to know about these things. I'm speaking mostly to fathers with kids on either arm and panicky.) All the major hotels around Union Square have public facilities off the lobby; the larger stores have facilities on every other floor. Don't be shy; just barge right in; even the smaller stores will accommodate.

As for food, there are many snack bars and quick lunch places in the downtown shopping area. I might recommend two for the parent minding the kids. BLUM'S in MACY'S, across from Union Square, has great, gooey pastries, sundaes, and sodas; the NOBLE FRANKFURTER, up Powell just across from Sutter Street (two blocks from Union Square) has all kinds of hot dogs, wursts, and hamburgers (free sauerkraut) for the hungry child—and beer for Dad or Mom.

Union Street

UNION STREET, between Steiner and Gough Streets, has some of the most interesting and varied shopping available in San Francisco. The shops are literally beyond description (there are over a hundred different shops in this six-block stretch), including antiques, clothing, museum-quality collectables, posters, and African safari gear and tours. Try to do this street without any pressure because it is a sheer delight to browse. Nearby are three great places for kids—two of them tourist attractions in themselves.

If you want to reach it by bus, walk up to Sutter Street at Stockton and catch either the No. 30 Stockton or the No. 45 Van Ness–Sutter. The No. 30 will take you along Union. The No. 45 will take you along Chestnut, four blocks away (short blocks) and get you closer to the Exploratorium and the Yacht Harbor. To drive, go out Geary to Van Ness, right on Van Ness to Lombard, left off Lombard at either Fillmore or Steiner Street. I mention public transportation because parking on and around Union Street is murder. There are several parking garages in the neighborhood, but it's no guarantee that you'll find a parking slot even there.

Union Street has many confection shops, snack bars, and restaurants. Near it on Lombard are the franchise places, such as Doggie Diner and Jack in the Box, and there are many delicatessens and groceries where a picnic can be put together without any trouble. Adults and the older kids find Union Street fascinating—because it is a fascinating street. It is, though, a street that adults find more fascinating than children do, so keep that in mind.

FUNSTON PARK. At Buchanan and Chestnut Streets. Walk down Fillmore Street from Union to Chestnut (four short blocks) and turn right. The park begins two blocks to your right. It's a large park with a great toddler's play area at Laguna and Chestnut, another four blocks up. It also has tennis courts and baseball fields. There is a public library here if you want to go in and sit or read stories to the little kids. One of the interesting things you might want to look at is the ingenious golf driving range—as short as two living rooms. You can swat the ball as hard as you want and the balls are stopped by a curtain of old, worn-out fire hoses—a clever and cheap arrangement to help you perfect your swing.

THE PALACE OF FINE ARTS AND EXPLORATORIUM. At Baker and Beach Streets. The whole family should visit this. (See Chapter 10.)

MARINA GREEN AND THE YACHT HARBOR. At Marina Boulevard. See Chapter 8. The whole family should also visit this.

THE CANNERY. GHIRARDELLI SQUARE. Both are covered in Chapter 2. Both are mouth-watering collections of great shopping. It's easier to deal with children there than the other two great shopping areas in the city.

8

The Yacht Harbor

THE SAN FRANCISCO Yacht Harbor and the Marina Green are not usually listed by the city as a major tourist attraction, but they are indeed. To get there, go out Geary Street to Van Ness Avenue, turn right, and follow the Golden Gate Bridge signs onto Lombard Street. Then get in the right lane and turn right on Fillmore to Marina Boulevard. It runs into the Marina Green Park. Turn left and keep in the right lane. You'll see the boats to your right, and, where the whole road sweeps to the left, turn to your right onto the road to the breakwater that forms the Yacht Harbor.

Here is one of the few places in the country where the average person can get a good look at the big sailing and motor yachts of the rich. In other cities with people rich enough to own ocean-going yachts, the yacht harbors are well hidden away from the public in their own special yachting places. Here, the yacht harbor is right off a main street, and you can check out the yachts from all angles.

To add to the enjoyment, there is a small sandy beach where kids can play.

To detract from the enjoyment, especially if you have your own runabout on Duck Lake back home, when you see these magnificent ocean-worthy sailors and motor palaces, you aren't apt to think your own is so hot any more. But then again, what you're looking at, the sail boats and motor yachts, cost in the neighborhood of a thousand dollars per running foot. But it's a great place for kids and certainly has inspired more daydreams of mighty ocean adventures than any other place in the city.

9

The San Francisco Zoo

By Car:
Drive a block up Geary to Mason, turn left down to Market and turn right on Market Street (and the detours) up over the hill past Twin Peaks and down to where it meets Sloat Boulevard—you'll make a half-right there. Follow the signs. Sloat Boulevard will take you to the zoo—it's on your left immediately before you drive into the ocean.
Public Transportation:
Walk down to Market and catch the L Taraval–Zoo streetcar. This is probably the best way to go with kids because it includes a wonderful streetcar ride, with a trip through a long tunnel. (See Chapter 17.)

The SAN FRANCISCO ZOO is not as grand as the Bronx, San Diego, or St. Louis zoos, but it's still a fine place. It's certainly better than the Washington, D.C., zoo, if you want a comparison—and, curiously has something in common with the zoo at the nation's capital. The two giant pandas there from China were exchanged for two musk oxen from the San Francisco Zoo.

There are some special things to see here: the primate area, with family groups of gorillas, orangutans, and chimpanzees on separate islands; pygmy hippos;

white rhinoceros. An "Elephant Train" will give you a grand tour of the zoo for a modest price, letting you see the layout and mark places where you want to go back and linger. For the children up to about eight, there are some small rides, including a merry-go-round and a steam train ride. The zoo has a great playground and lots of picnic areas—the playground furniture includes an old Southern Pacific steam engine and a cable car. For mothers with small children, there is an ornate mother's shelter where mothers with little children can relax. The zoo rents strollers (and wheel chairs as well).

Near the playground-rides-picnic area is a BABY ZOO–STORYLAND area. For a modest admission, you can wander through, climb on, and slide down concrete and fiberglas settings of the Mother Goose rhymes. Most important is the Baby Zoo, where young animals from the zoo (and the zoo is big, so there are always little exotic creatures) can be looked at and touched. There is a small menagerie of tame and friendly animals to pet and feed—it's a delightful corner of the zoo. Snack bars are found in several places, so you don't have to bring a picnic lunch if you don't want to. One marvelous feature of the children's zoo is that birthday parties can be arranged there for groups of twelve or more. For information call 661-1699.

At the end of Sloat, where it meets the Great Highway, is a stretch of Ocean Beach called locally "Taraval Beach," though Taraval Street is some blocks north. From here south, there are all kinds of good things to do—besides walking on the beach. Immediately out of the parking area, you'll see layers of black sand. This is gold-bearing sand, and you can pan for gold here. From here to Thornton Beach State Park and south to Mussel Rock (about four miles of beach walking) you'll find fossil sand dollars and, if you're lucky, fossil whale teeth or camel bones. (see Chapter 19.)

10

Museums

MANY people shy away even from the word "museum" because it is a dry, dusty word. It is to their loss. Look to the five- to twelve-year-olds. They're intensely interested in "old stuff," "new stuff," and just plain "stuff." They're natural museum curators. They collect things and like to see collections. The dictionary definition of "museum" is not "endless rows of glass cabinets full of dead stuff," but "a place where objects of value or lasting interest are collected and displayed." It takes money to gather together items of value or special interest; it takes wide patronage (again money) to house and display these objects; and that's the reason that most museums are found only in large cities. It is the reason to visit them when you're touring the city and the Bay area.

The museums here are very special. There are fine-art museums and natural-history museums. There are specialized museums that have to be seen to be believed. Some are chock-full of gold dust, nuggets, and coins; four ships here are museums—as well as being museum pieces in themselves. I know of no other place in the country where you can see displays of riveted buffalo-hide fire hoses or the working papers required of nineteenth century Chinese immigrants. This is an area rich in museums.

Most of the museums listed here are a treat for the

whole family. The great majority are free; those that charge admission are well worth the tariff—which is usually modest. Some of the museums are described in other sections of the book, but they're all listed here. There will be some that you'll want to pass, but some that you shouldn't, even if you're here only a short time. Look at the description before starting out. In each case, I'll try to indicate the age of children interested in each of them. Also, I'll try to give good selling points for each. Lord knows, if you travel by car from the Middle West, North, or South to San Francisco, your kids will be pestering you to death to stop to see collections of objects of interest or lasting value, such as: *Snakes!* THE BIGGEST AND MOST POISONOUS SNAKE IN THE WORLD! GHOST TOWN! PAN FOR YOUR OWN GOLD! OLD-TIME RAILROAD!

These too are museums, but paltry things compared to what we have to offer.

Major Museums

THE DE YOUNG MEMORIAL MUSEUM. Golden Gate Park. Daily, 10 AM–5 PM. Free.

This museum has recognized masterpieces of fine art; Cellini sculpture, El Greco and Rubens paintings, and more. It is the official museum of the city in that any major touring show is likely to be shown here. Lots of old stuff for the kids—suits of armor, reconstructed period rooms, a mummy. (For a full description, see Chapter 3.)

THE SAN FRANCISCO CENTER OF ASIAN ART AND CULTURE. Golden Gate Park. A wing adjoined to the De Young, it has the same hours. Free.

As I said, it's a little rich, but there's enough nearby to entertain little ones for the adults to trade off and get a glimpse of a truly magnificent collection. (See Chapter 3.)

CALIFORNIA ACADEMY OF SCIENCES. Golden Gate Park. Opposite the De Young on the Music Concourse.

One of the most interesting museums in the city. Includes Natural History sections, the Steinhart Aquarium, the Morrison Planetarium, the Hall of Minerals, and exhibits on space, time, and oil lamps from Biblical days. This is one of the major cultural attractions of the city and should be visited by every visitor. All ages enjoy it, even babes in arms. (See Chapter 3.)

PALACE OF THE LEGION OF HONOR. In Lincoln Park, 35th Ave. and Clement Street. Daily, 10 AM–5 PM. Free. To get there, drive out Geary Boulevard to 35th Avenue and turn right. One block and you are at the entrance of Lincoln Park (you'll see the golf course). The museum is at the top of the hill.

The building is a copy of the Palace of the Legion of Honor in Paris. It was one of the many donations to the city by the Spreckels family (of the sugar fortune). This museum was a pet of the late, wonderful, Mrs. Alma Spreckels. When she was young, she was a friend of Auguste Rodin, the great French sculptor, and here you'll see more Rodin than anywhere else in the country. Inside there is an excellent collection of fine art, and the Auchenback Foundation for Graphic Arts is one of the best graphic-arts collections anywhere. It is a sedate, rather elegant museum where you are likely to be frowned at if your kids aren't under control. When your little boys get fretful, send them outside—there are plenty of good balustrades to climb on and a beautiful lawn on which to romp. The museum grounds offer some of the best views of the approach to the Golden Gate and the bridge in town—a great place for photographs.

SAN FRANCISCO MUSEUM OF ART. Van Ness and McAllister, across from City Hall. Tuesday–Friday 10

AM–10 PM; Saturday, 10 AM–5 PM; Sunday, 1 PM–
5 PM. Free (admission charge for special exhibits.)

This museum is a must for teen-age kids interested
in art. It concentrates on "modern" art and the latest
trends in contemporary art. There are some recent
masters represented, such as Matisse and Cezanne,
but the largest area is devoted to what is happening
now. If you don't know much about modern art, here
is an opportunity at least to *see* what is being done
now, even if you don't understand it. There is an
excellent shop at the museum where you can find
good buys in books, prints, and photos. Even smaller
children seem to like the sculpture they can touch
and the kinetic things they can make move.

CALIFORNIA GEOLOGY MUSEUM. Ferry Building.
Monday–Friday, 8 AM–5 PM; first Saturday of every
month, 10 AM–noon. Free.

An excellent museum for the whole family. Great
collection of gold and minerals. California minerals
displayed county by county. Rockhounds shouldn't
miss it. Good, cheap books on where to find gold and
the whats and whys of earthquakes, geological maps,
and so on.

THE OLD MINT. Fifth and Mission Streets. Hours at
this writing are Tuesday–Saturday, 10 AM–4 PM.

This is San Francisco's newest major museum. This
old mint was built in the middle of the 1870s to replace an older facility that couldn't handle the coinage demands of the developing West. It's operated by
the Treasury Department Bureau of Engraving. Permitted to fall into disrepair for many years, it is now
in the process of restoration to its once glorious, almost
flamboyant magnificence. It's one of the few buildings in the downtown area to survive the earthquake-
fire. Shortly before the 'quake, wells were dug in the
courtyard, and, when the water mains broke, it was

one of the few independent sources of water downtown. Dedicated employees manned the pumps and hoses and saved the building.

It opened July 1, 1973, and at this writing is still in the process of sorting itself out. The interior of the building is beautiful. It's a joy to walk through and admire the craftsmanship that went into the elegant hardwood floors, the beautiful plasterwork and gilding, the cabinet work and woodcarving. It was a suitable place for the hundreds of millions of dollars of gold and silver to be stamped into hard money. Here is a building that our great-grandparents enjoyed—and so will our great-grandchildren.

There is an interesting display of old minting machinery and equipment, including a stamping machine that will convert a bronze slug (about the size of a silver dollar, and costing a dollar), with a satisfying chuff-*whump,* before your very eyes, into a very nice memento of the mint. Since the museum is new, all the exhibits are not yet in place. According to personnel, the eventual aim is to make this the finest numismatic museum in America. Even as it is now, it's a very fine place to visit.

FORT POINT. The Presidio, beneath the Toll Plaza of Golden Gate Bridge. Daily, 10 AM–5 PM. Free.

To get there, follow the same directions given before, turning into the View Area, just before you get to the Toll Plaza. Instead of turning into the parking lot, though, follow the road to the Presidio, turning left down the hill at the first stop sign. From there, follow the signs.

Fort Point was built to guard the Golden Gate against attacks from the Confederacy. It's the only stone and brick fort west of the Mississippi, and it's something to see. The walls are immensely thick—it's a good chance to examine the masonry skills of a century ago. In all its history, the guns of Fort Point have never been fired in anger, but it has acted as a talis-man for San Francisco, guarding us from the Confed-eracy, the Spanish in 1898, the Germans, the Japa-nese, the North Koreans, the Chinese, and North Vietnamese. It's like the old joke about the Eskimo who wore a shoe around his neck. "Why do you wear that?" he was asked. "It keeps the alligators away." "You dummy, there aren't any alligators within three thousand miles of here!" "See," said the Eskimo. "It works!"

This museum is for the whole family. You can in-spect the officers' and men's quarters, the gun ports, the stockade—the meanest few jail cells I've ever seen. There are several examples of antique artillery in the courtyard. The views from the gun ports are spectacular. There is a small museum of period mili-tary equipment and ordinance right off the entrance. One of the guides, who knows everything about the place, is dressed in antique army uniform. (Officers in those days wore feathers in their hats—a dashing touch.) Look especially at the circular granite stair-cases. All pivot from a central built-in pole—as mod-ern as tomorrow. Be warned that it is right at the point of the Golden Gate, which means that it is apt to be cold and windy. Take sweaters or windbreakers. From Fort Point, you get your finest opportunity to examine the roadway and anchorage of the Golden Gate Bridge. Sport fishermen note: the breakwater of Fort Point is one of the very finest places in the Bay to catch striped bass when they're running. Don't miss this place; it's special. Good for all ages.

San Francisco Maritime State Historic Park. Foot of Hyde Street on Fisherman's Wharf.

These are four antique ships, museum pieces in themselves that are also museums. Suitable for all ages, this is not to be missed because you'll find its like nowhere else. (See Chapter 2.)

THE EXPLORATORIUM. Old Palace of Fine Arts. Baker and Beach Streets. Wednesday–Sunday, 1 PM– 5 PM. Free.

To get there, go out Geary, Van Ness, and Lombard as if you were going to the Golden Gate Bridge. On Lombard Street, keep in the right lane. As you approach the Presidio, turn right down any of the streets after you pass Fillmore. Divisadero, Broderick, or Baker are all good; drive to Beach Street and turn left. You'll see the Palace of Fine Arts ahead of you. The Exploratorium is in the right wing.

Before we look at the Exploratorium, a word about the building, the Palace of Fine Arts. This is a replica of the last structure that remained from the Panama-Pacific Exposition of 1915—a world's fair that purported to celebrate the opening of the Panama Canal, but really showed how magnificently San Francisco had recovered from the 1906 earthquake. The earthquake-fire destroyed much of the city, but such was the energy of the rebuilding that the city was in a position to host a world's fair only nine years later. Remember that this was before the development of much heavy-duty equipment, bulldozers, fleets of heavy trucks, back hoes. Nearly all the water, sewer, and gas lines had to be repaired or rebuilt; streets, as well as cable-car, streetcar, and railroad lines, had to be repaired; and this is not to speak of rebuilding almost the whole downtown area from scratch. Much of the rebuilding was hand work, muscle work, and it's amazing that so much was accomplished in such a short time. To show off their city, the San Franciscans launched this Panama-Pacific Exposition, which was a gaudy thing indeed. The land in the Marina District on which it was built was mostly filled ground, with the express purpose of using the land for residential purposes after the Exposition was over.

As in all such world's fairs, the buildings were temporary structures, built to last only through the few months of the Exposition. The original Palace of Fine

Arts, like the others, was chicken wire, lath, and plaster over flimsy supporting steel girders. After the Exposition, all the other buildings were torn down on schedule, but this building, by the famed architect Bernard Maybeck, was so lovely that it, and its lagoon, was preserved by the city as park land. Incredibly, the building endured . . . and endured. It was originally designed as a Roman ruin, and as the years went by, it became more and more beautiful. Planned to last less than a year, it stood for more than forty, despite salt fog, rains, and vandalism. But as bits of plaster fell off the walls and vandals laid waste to the structure (one dummy knocked off the heads of the ladies on top of the building with baseball bats), it was finally condemned as unsafe to all concerned and slated to be torn down. Walter Johnson, a local millionaire and a lover of the city, put up a huge amount of money, which was matched by a local bond issue, and reconstruction began. The original molds for the statuary of the building—again an incredible stroke of luck: they'd been sitting in a warehouse for all these years—were found, and the Palace of Fine Arts again rose. This time, the building was made of permanent materials, such as reinforced concrete, keeping the original coloring. What you now see is a piece of the past saved just because it was too pretty to lose.

The Exploratorium itself is a collection of exhibits that, through mechanical, physical, and technical devices, trick you, test you, and let you discover the complications that have been discovered in this complicated world. In one machine, you see an image before your eyes. You reach to touch it, and your hand passes completely through it! In another exhibit, the light of the sun here plays a musical instrument. In an aluminum-walled, strobe-lighted room, you find that the wiggle of your fingers is not a simple act. There are machines to test your eyes, your ears, and your body in ways you'll find delightful. One of the best things is the display of holograms. These are laser trick photographs on a two-dimensional sheet of plastic—but when you move your head, you can look around the corners and see things in back of the things in front. Amazing! Here also are replicas of such things as Alan Sheppard's Freedom 7 space capsule—a tiny thing—explanations of nuclear energy, and more. It is a place for the whole family and one of the most amusing, entertaining, and instructive museums in San Francisco. Kids can run wild here with no fuss—and they will.

The Exploratorium is close to the Yacht Harbor and Union Street. It's a good two-hour place for kids if one or the other of the parents wants to shop.

Special Exhibits and Private Museums

It was a hard choice to divide the San Francisco museums between major and special. The major museums listed above are all funded by the city, state, or federal governments. A few listed below are also city funded, but most are privately sustained, either by businesses or by private membership, or are half commercial, half funded by interested patrons. All museums are collections of special stuff, collected and displayed by people who are intensely interested in preserving them. Some of the smaller museums are more interesting in their own way than the big ones. In every case you'll find them delightful. As I said, this is a pack-rat city, chock-full of good things.

SAN FRANCISCO MARITIME MUSEUM. Foot of Polk Street in Aquatic Park. Daily, 10 AM–5 PM. Free.

A fine collection of commercial shipping memorabilia (as opposed to military ships). Antique figureheads, exhibits of rigging and machinery, antique navigational equipment, scale models of ships, and sometimes special exhibits, like the scrimshaw carvings on whale ivory that are being shown at this writing. It is a maritime nostalgia museum that is fitting to this long-time port. It's a "man against the sea" kind of place that doesn't have an exhibit of the newest container ships or LASH boats (they utilize few sailors and fewer dock workers), but it use to proudly display the *Mermaid,* a twenty-foot sailboat that carried the intrepid adventurer Haurie from Japan to San Francisco.

It's a good place to go with your teen-agers to orient yourselves before you see the Historic Ships State Park down the street or go aboard the *Balclutha.* It's not too large, so the littler kids won't suffer when you tour it. (See Chapter 2.)

THE BALCLUTHA. Pier 43. Fisherman's Wharf. (See Chapter 2.)

This is absolutely one of the finest museums in town. My five-year-old got a little bored because there's so much to see, but from seven or so up, they can get involved in this last ship to sail around the Horn in a regular cargo capacity. The three decks are full of interesting things. There is an admission charge, but it's well worth it. Nowhere else will you have a chance to walk the decks of a "Round the Horner" and get the feel of what it was to be a deepwater sailor in the days of sail.

WELLS FARGO HISTORY ROOM. 420 Montgomery Street. Banker's hours, Monday–Friday, 10 AM–3 PM. Free. To get there, walk down Post Street to Montgomery, turn left, and walk four blocks to the address.

Wells Fargo is a historic name in California. It was one of the first banking systems to offer banking security at the Mother Lode mines, express transport to shipping points, and security in San Francisco. Wells Fargo's early business life dealt with gold, bandits, and brave men who captured them. The Wells Fargo museum is thus chock-full of gold of every description, from each of the centers of the Mother Lode, and Pony Express saddle bags, and great big solid silver turnip watches, awarded to the bandit-catchers, and famous pistols that shot famous bandits and . . . everything exciting! Wells Fargo, being so history conscious, has a very fine collection of pamphlets and brochures—on early California place names, for example—that are free for the asking.

The first thing you'll wonder is how they got the huge Concord stagecoach in the door. I asked, and they said they didn't know. When you look at it and see if it could be dismantled and sneaked through, you'll also be confused. The only conclusion is that they built the building around it. It's a private museum, but it's one of the most exciting in the town.

BANK OF CALIFORNIA GOLD AND COIN ROOM. 400 California Street (corner of California and Sansome). To get there, walk down Post to Market, left on Market to Sansome, and left to California. Monday–Friday, 10 AM–3 PM. Free.

This is a very interesting collection of Western American monies, lots of gold and silver coins (and bars of gold), as well as paper currency from British Columbia south to California and east to what is now Utah. It's a good lesson in how money becomes and what money is—a mystery approaching theological speculation, which people have a hard time understanding.

Here's a short explanation. United States currency (coins especially) was always in short supply in the Western half of the continent in the early days, since the West was far from the places where coins were minted. There was incredible wealth here in raw products—lumber and cattle, for example—and in gold and silver fresh from the mines. But there were few coins of the various denominations, nickels, dimes, quarters, dollars, and the five-dollar, ten-dollar, and twenty-dollar gold pieces that people needed for their daily business. When few people were in the territory, money didn't matter much. The barter system worked fairly well. A trading ship would pull in with a load of cloth, manufactured goods, pots, pans, axes, and these would be traded for a load of cattle hides, for example (as in the book *Two Years Before the Mast.*)

With the gold rush and the development of the Pacific Northwest, and the western territories of Utah, Colorado, Wyoming, the barter system broke down. Some kind of money was needed to ease small purchases and pay wages. The pinch of gold dust became a fairly common unit of value, good for a haircut or a drink at a bar but one man's pinch wasn't the same as another's. That's where the old saying "He's good in a pinch" came from. A fat-thumbed man was more valued than a skinny-fingered man because he could pinch up more gold dust.

What you see in this collection are efforts from assaying offices, banking companies, and heads of government to take up the slack until United States government mints moved West. There are at least fifteen different private coinages and bank notes from Alaska, Oregon Territory, California, Colorado Territory, and the State of Deseret (which is now Utah). The latter is probably the most interesting. To provide cash, the Mormon state printed one-, two-, and three-dollar bank notes. Each of these bills was personally signed by Brigham Young and countersigned by three bishops of the church—to provide a sound foundation for their worth. This provides a built-in protection against devalued currency. You can write only so much money before writer's cramp sets in.

The private coinage you see here was very useful, but also had its own problems. The coins put out by the different banking or assay houses varied in the weight and fineness of gold in each coin, so they all weren't the same value. It wasn't until the mints came

West that everyone knew that every ten-dollar gold piece was worth exactly ten dollars.

This is a very interesting place, fine for all to visit, but a must if any of your kids collect coins.

SOCIETY OF CALIFORNIA PIONEERS. 465 McAllister Street, near City Hall. Monday–Friday, 10 AM–4 PM. Free.

This small but elegant, museum exhibits many fine items of Californiana. The items in the constantly changing display seem always to capture the essence of the history of the state. Once I saw Indian artifacts; the beautiful silver service of an early Spanish governor; brass draft-beer taps from memorable early saloons; fused coins and glass from the earthquake-fire; election flags, posters and buttons from turn-of-the-century California elections; and a Spanish cutlass from the early days of exploration. With it was a magic-lantern slide show of the Panama-Pacific Exposition. It's perhaps a little rich for little kids—especially those from out of state—but should be of great interest to those California children studying state history in school. All adults would enjoy it.

FIREMAN'S PIONEER MUSEUM. Presidio near Pine. Pine Street is one way out and ends at Presidio Avenue. Turn left at the end of Pine and you're there. Monday–Friday, 1 PM–4 PM. Free. Group tours on weekends by special arrangement.

San Francisco is a fire-conscious town and its firemen are highly regarded. The winds that blow constantly from the Pacific could whip any small fire in this closely packed city into a major conflagration if our fire department weren't so highly-trained and efficient. The department follows a practice of over-kill. Where, in other cities, only one fire company would respond to a given call, we send out enough men to stomp out the fire with their very boots. The men respond immediately and swarm on the fire so that in the Sunset, for example, where there are some

370 square blocks of houses all touching each other on the narrow lots, the house in the middle may be gutted, but those on either side are rarely scorched. As you drive through the city, you'll notice round brick circles in the intersections of the downtown blocks. These are cisterns of reserve water in case another earthquake strikes, and, like the last big one, breaks the water mains.

This museum is a repository of antique fire-fighting equipment, mementos, and San Francisco history. can Legion Post here. Even though they were exhibit include two hand-drawn manual pumpers dating from the 1850s (the days of the volunteer fire brigades); a horse-drawn steam pumper; a 1908 Ahrens-Fox piston pumper; and a 1908 high-pressure battery and hose tender. There are a chief's buggy and other smaller pieces. They are fascinating because, like railroad equipment, they are huge and beautifully crafted.

Along the walls are display cases with all kinds of good stuff: leather fire buckets; glass water grenades; speaking trumpets; items of firemen's uniform; an excellent exhibition of the evolution of the fire hose (in the old days, the hose was of riveted buffalo hide); and much more. The men in charge of the museum have a wealth of knowledge about all the items on display, old fires, and San Francisco.

They let the little kids ring the bells on the fire engines and touch the equipment—as long as they don't climb on it too dangerously. You must sign an insurance waiver when you go in, in case there's an accident (the equipment is exciting, so don't let your kids go wild and run into something). It's small, but you'll find you're in there for an hour. Good for the whole family.

SAN FRANCISCO CABLE-CAR MUSEUM. Washington and Mason Streets.

The cable-car barn fascinates everyone. It is a working museum and here you'll see the huge machinery and flywheels that move the cables that pull the cable cars over the hills of San Francisco. From the balcony overlooking the floor of the shop you can not only watch the immense, gaudily painted driving mechanism of the cable-car system, but also see what a machine shop looked like in the olden days. A single power source, through a complicated web of overhead belts and pulleys, operates grinders, lathes, milling machines, and who knows what else.

The viewing balcony has the original 1873 cable car on display, models of others, and interesting facts about our unique transportation system. In the cable-car barns in the same building, but around and up the hill, you will see cable cars from discontinued lines; very nice displays such as the gripping device that enables the cable cars to catch the cable, ride it, and let go; and reserve parts for the ongoing process of repairing the cars in use.

OCTAGON HOUSE. 2645 Gough Street. First Sunday and second and fourth Thursdays of every month, 1 PM–4 PM. Free.

This eight-sided house is an architectural curiosity dating from 1861. Even before the geodesic dome and "modern" round houses, there was much early experimentation of departures from the standard four-corner structure. George Washington designed and built a twelve-sided barn on his Mount Vernon estate. The idea was to provide more window space and natural lighting in the days when artificial lighting—candles, oil lamps—was poor and costly.

The hours are odd because it's the headquarters of the California branch of the Colonial Dames of America. It's elegantly furnished with excellent examples of Chippendale, Hepplewhite, Sheraton, and Queen Anne furniture, but it's not for little kids. Adults who are collectors or want to swap genealogies with the volunteers might find it interesting.

THE CALIFORNIA HISTORICAL SOCIETY. 2090 Jackson Street. Tuesday–Saturday, 10 AM–4 PM. Free.

This is another interesting museum that is not for most kids. The administrative headquarters of the society usually has an exhibit of Western genre paintings, but the most interesting thing about the museum is the place itself. It was the old Whittier mansion, and fine craftsmanship went into the moldings, flooring, plasterwork, and cabinets, that can hardly be duplicated today.

CHINESE HISTORICAL SOCIETY OF AMERICA. 17 Adler Street. Tuesday–Sunday, 1 PM–5 PM. Free.

Adler Street is a short alley between Grant and Columbus, a few steps south of Broadway. A walk through Chinatown gives you a glimpse of a culture that is truly foreign to Americans and Europeans (see Chapter 11), and that's rare enough. Even rarer, though, is a look at how a culture, entirely foreign, excluded and despised, worked within another culture. Preserved in this museum are memorabilia from the hundred-plus years of the Chinese in America—the American Chinese. You must remember that the Chinese were excluded and "ghettoized" for a very long period. The Hero's Grove stone in Golden Gate Park that lists the World War I San Francisco dead doesn't include one Chinese name on the long roster —even though there is an American-Chinese American Legion Post here. Even though they were excluded from the mainstream of pioneer American life, they were an integral part of the development of the West. The things passed on by the families, saved and displayed in this museum, show a pride in the Chinese contribution to this history.

In the museum, for instance, there is a genuine Chinese sampan—built in Marin County across the Bay by the shrimp fishermen there. (Dried Bay shrimp was a common export item to China in those early days). From the Mother Lode comes a finely crafted wooden wheelbarrow—no metal, all pieces doweled together. The Chinese as laborers are shown in the garden of the museum in a portion of a rough stone wall brought here. (The Chinese cleared the vinyard land of Sonoma County of the stones covering it.) A Chinese cook in a northern mining camp broke his only cooking spoon; the miners welded it with the most available metal—gold. These things were saved, as well as their working papers and a wealth of photographs of pioneer Chinese-Americans of the West. Exotic things are seen here as well, such as an antique Mandarin silk cloak, slippers for the bound "lily feet" of aristocratic ladies; opium-smoking paraphernalia; sections of Buddhist and Taoist temples; but most striking and memorable are the mundane things.

You will see, for example, the contents of an immigrant Chinese man's trunk, stored and never reclaimed. He included all the things he thought he would need in this foreign land—paramount was a china tea service, pot and cups. Like no other museum, this small one gives you a real idea of what it means to be a stranger in a foreign land, an unfriendly foreign land. When Chinatown was destroyed in the fire that followed the earthquake, people flocked to see the secret tunnels that were supposed to riddle the ghetto. None were found. Instead, you'll see here appeals from the San Francisco Chinese to other Chinese-Americans in the West for donations—a relief fund. They had to do it among themselves because they didn't expect much from the local governments.

This museum is for all ages. It's primarily operated by the Society, so be sure to put a good donation in the box. This museum should show other minorities how to present their contributions to the culture of the new world.

SAN FRANCISCO AFRICAN-AMERICAN HISTORICAL AND CULTURAL SOCIETY. 680 McAllister Street. Monday–Friday, noon–5 PM. Free.

Like the Chinese-American museum, this is a people-proud collection of black culture. Antique African carvings and pottery and modern African art and clothing are balanced by a display of proud accomplishment by black Americans in a society always hostile to blacks. An exhibit of Dr. George Washington Carver's fantastic utilization of the peanut (he was one of the first biochemists to explore fully the use of a field crop as a chemical resource) is especially interesting. There is a listing of solid accomplishments by black architects (the laying out of Washington, D.C.); black doctors (the first open-heart surgery in America); black inventors, businessmen, and sports and entertainment figures. The museum is small, but growing. Little ones won't appreciate it as much as older kids.

WORLD OF OIL. Standard Oil Building, 555 Market Street. Monday–Friday, 10 AM–4 PM. Free.

A great deal of money went into this specialized museum, which shows the complicated processes of finding oil, drilling for it, and turning crude oil into its many components. There are good things to see here, such as the examples of the huge drill bits used in the digging, the geology of oil, and the motion picture that you see when you first go in, which explains how oil came to be. For some reason, though, there's something missing. The first thing that comes to mind is the lack of pride—it's a presentation, a commercial, instead of a proud display of a rather exotic industry. Oil is money and nowhere is there a mention of the glorious feeling one must get when you strike oil and are suddenly rich. The two bank museums that have gold displays haven't neglected this. There are no displays of the boom towns, no photographs of men made millionaires and billionaires through the business, no hint of the glamour, adventure, or hardship of the industry, and that's a pity. But it's eminently understandable, of course, in an era when all energy moguls appear suspect.

This museum is mostly for older kids and adults

interested in the technical aspects of the petroleum industry.

JOSEPHINE D. RANDALL JUNIOR MUSEUM. Museum Way at Corona Heights Park. Tuesday–Saturday, 10 AM–5 PM; Sunday, noon–4:30 PM. Free. To get there, follow Geary to Mason Street and turn left down to Market. Turn right on Market and drive out to the entrance of the Twin Peaks tunnel. Turn right on Castro, up the hill, left on Fourteenth Street, up the hill to Roosevelt Way, and left again. You'll see a large meadow within a chain-link fence. Turn left onto Museum Way to the museum.

This is a combination view, playground, and museum. The Josephine D. Randall Junior Museum is the finest of all the "children's zoos and museums" in the Bay area for closely examining and handling small wild animals. The museum is a complex of workshops for kids and teen-agers. There are corners devoted to art, ceramics, automotive engineering, woodworking, archaeology–geology–paleontology, a huge model railroad layout, nature study–ecology–conservation, and more. The living creatures within the building include skunks, rabbits, foxes, coatis, raccoons, mice, rats, ferrets; mynah birds, owls, hawks, eagles, and other, smaller fliers; lizards, tortoises, and a variety of snakes. Most of these beasts are tame to the touch or can be safely held. Now *this* is a grand place to take smaller children, but everyone enjoys it. I have a special affection for it because a mynah bird here taught my son, when he was a year and a half, to say "hello." He only said "Hi" before we took him there, and he and the bird got into a solemn, ten-minute conversation of "Hello," "Hi"; "Hello," "Hi"; "Hello," "Hello." It was an unusual, and funny, example of beast teaching man to talk, and we cherish the memory.

Outside the museum are the many attractions that constitute Corona Heights Park. There are playgrounds, tennis courts, and running room on the slopes surrounding the two bald spires of rock that offer a fine view. Of special interest to rockhounds, and interesting to all, are the geological curiosities. This area lies within an ancient fault line that ran from Hunter's Point to Telegraph Hill. There is a hundred-foot rock cliff here polished to mirror smoothness by the movements of a hundred earthquakes eons ago (technically called "slickensides"). It's beneath the level of the museum and is best seen when you come up. Instead of turning left from Castro at Fourteenth, turn left at Beaver Street. There is a path leading down from the heights so you can see it either way, but the first stop is best if you have little kids.

Corona Heights is one of the finest views in the city. It's a climbing view, in that you have to hoist yourselves up a rocky pathway to the top—holding on to the rocks, touching the viewpoint as it were. It's a steep but easy climb, suitable for three-year-olds and grandmas, and very satisfying. Not many citizens or tourists know this is public park land, so you're likely to have the whole of the peak to yourselves.

MISSION DOLORES. Sixteenth and Dolores Streets. Daily, 10 AM–4 PM. Admission at this writing, 25¢.

The Mission Dolores is one of the most venerable places in San Francisco, a major tourist attraction. It's one of the chain of missions, founded under the supervision of Fra Junipero Serra, that stretched from San Diego to San Rafael. Although suitable for teen-agers and older kids who have studied American and California history, it's not too interesting to smaller kids except for a few points. The Mission was built by Indians and the very interesting ceiling decorations in the church were created by them. Along the walls are religious and secular artifacts from the 1780s on; the graveyard is full of Spanish, Mexican, and American California pioneers. Both the church and the grounds are small, and if it is in your itinerary, the little kids won't have too long a wait as you tour it.

CALIFORNIA RAILWAY MUSEUM. Rio Vista Junction.

Open Saturday, noon–5 PM, Sunday, noon–6 PM; Holidays, noon–5 PM. Free. This is just a shade beyond our fifty-mile limit, but is a must for railroad, streetcar, and interurban buffs. To get there, take the Bay Bridge and Highway 80, as if you were going to Sacramento. At Fairfield, take the State Route 12 turnoff to Rio Vista-Lodi. About ten miles out of Fairfield, you'll cross the only railroad bridge on the road. The museum is immediately across it; then make an abrupt right. Driving time is about one hour from the Bay Bridge.

This collection of antique streetcars, trolleys, interurbans, cable cars; and some railroad stock has been (and is yet being) gathered by the Bay Area Electric Railroad Association. The membership that lovingly restores these old cars comes from all walks of life (my special thanks to Jack Cole, Manager of the North Beach Branch of the San Francisco Library who told me of its existence). You and your kids can climb on and examine cars of all shapes and vintages from New York "El" cars to the San Francisco–Chico Interurban; from the Iron Monsters of the San Francisco trolley system to streetcars from all over America. Many of the streetcars and electric locomotives are in operating condition and for a small fee (the cars operate on Sundays), you can again ride on wicker seats.

The museum-bookstore has (at least it appears so) every book, pamphlet, and brochure in print about electric and steam cars that moved on rails. Railroad souvenirs, engineer caps, bandanas, and watch fobs with famous lines logos, can be bought here as well as a wealth of railroad postcards. There are a few picnic tables, but the kids might prefer to go back to Fairfield's very fine city park that you passed on your way in or continue to Rio Vista which is right on the Sacramento River.

11

Chinatown

ROUGHLY the area along Grant Avenue from Bush Street to Broadway, between Stockton and Kearny Streets. From Union Square on foot, walk down Post Street to Grant Avenue and turn left. Chinatown begins two blocks farther on. By auto, drive down Post and left on Kearny. Park in the Portsmouth Square public parking garage at Clay Street.

San Francisco's Chinatown is a very special place and a must for every visitor. It's the largest Chinese community outside the Orient and, as such, the closest thing to visiting the Orient without actually going there. It's a large area, some twenty square blocks with about thirty thousand residents.

Originally, Chinatown was a ghetto in the dictionary sense—a place of exclusion and containment. Until relatively recently, Chinese citizens were discouraged from living anywhere outside Chinatown. Now, of course, there are few neighborhoods in the city without Chinese families. But Chinatown remains, and probably always will, the heart and cultural center for the Chinese community. The shops and groceries that sell the special vegetables, meats, and cooking equipment used in Chinese cooking are here; the schools, social clubs, newspapers, and places of worship (Catholic, Protestant, Buddhist, and Taoist) are here; and, for many Chinese living outside Chinatown, it's an excellent place to make a living because it's a tourist attraction.

A visit to Chinatown is a grand cultural experience for you and your kids, but often much is missed because there is a tendency to get bogged down in the shops. Lord knows that Grant Avenue is a trap that way—shop after shop after shop. These shops do have great buys in souvenirs and such things as tea sets to send back to Grandma and Grandpa, but they aren't all of Chinatown. The following is a small guide through Chinatown, so you can see the best of it and catch the flavor that most tourists miss.

First, though, here are some answers to some commonly asked questions from kids. The first is "Why Chinatown?" The Chinese-Americans have been in this country since the early 1850s, when huge numbers of contract laborers were brought over to provide cheap muscle for the mines, farms, and railroads. The area recruited by the employers' agents was mostly around Canton, and the main dialect in Chinatown is Cantonese. Though many Chinese laborers went back home when their period of contract was up, many stayed, founding their own businesses (fishing, laundry, food processing, farming) or joining the lowest level of the labor pool—becoming household servants, cooks, and the like. They brought over their wives or sent back home for mail-order brides. The Chinese had greater cultural ties to the homeland than most other immigrant groups, and they retained their own language and ways much more than the Europeans because, unlike the others, the Chinese were systematically denied full acceptance into the American mainstream—denied citizenship and legally barred from many areas of work. This barring made them cling closer to the culture they brought with them—a rich and ancient one.

As the only large concentration of Orientals in America, Chinatown, even in the early days, was an exotic place to visit—a tourist attraction, and the city government rather felt the same thing; it was a place apart. This meant that most of the ordinary social services were denied—police protection; public schooling; care of the poor, sick, and old. Chinatown had to develop its own set of social institutions. Family Associations, "Tongs," were organized to care for those with the same last names (there were relatively few surnames in the area from which the majority of Chinatown residents originated). These associations provided employment services, schooling, social welfare, and a court system to settle business and personal differences within the family. Some vied for the control of the gambling, smuggling, and other vice within Chinatown. The struggle for control resulted in "Tong Wars" and increased the sinister mystique of the area. Gangsterism was so rampant that killers for hire, "highbinders" gathered daily around bulletin boards on which people who wanted to wipe out competition posted notices of how much they would pay for a specific killing. This made Chinatown even more exotic to the other San Franciscans and America. The diabolic Fu Manchu complex developed, and penny novels, movie serials, and newspaper articles abounded. All this time, of course, the average soul in Chinatown was scuffling to make a decent living for his family, educating his kids, and honoring his culture. When Chinatown burned during the earthquake, much of the mystique evaporated—there were no secret tunnels under the streets and the victims of the earthquake were sending appeals to fellow Chinese-Americans throughout the West and to the Manchu Dynasty back home for earthquake relief.

Although there were close ties to Chinese culture, it's not usually remembered that these weren't slavish ties to the antique Chinese government. It was in San Francisco that Sun Yat-sen and a strong group of followers formulated the overthrow of the corrupt

Manchu regime. The democracy of America, even though it didn't fully apply to the citizens of Chinatown, brought changes in the homeland.

As for the question, "Why still Chinatown—their own language, their own vegetables and culture?" the answer is, "Lucky for us non-Chinese, so we can see it." Chinese-Americans feel so strongly the worth of their own culture that even though some grandparents, certainly their parents, and most certainly *they* went to public schools, they still send their children to Chinese-language schools, after public-school hours, to get that instruction.

Start at Bush and Grant and walk up the hill. From here to a little beyond California Street are the larger Chinese emporiums. Here you will find the elegant stuff, teak furniture, bolts of exotic silks, truly fine porcelain, and the like. It is well to go into these shops to see what quality goods are available ($750 embroidered silk tablecloths, $2,500 antique porcelian figures, for example) so as to get some perspective when you come to the souvenir shops farther along the street. These shops are obviously for adults.

From California, the street tends to smaller shops, small businesses, and some grocery stores. The grocery stores are extremely interesting in that you'll see fruits and vegetables that will probably be new to you. You've undoubtedly eaten them, if you've ever had dinner in a Chinese restaurant, but the whole vegetables are seldom seen outside. The Chinese use a lot of vegetables in their cooking—meat has always been so expensive that it is used more as a flavoring agent and garnish than the main part. Don't be afraid to ask the clerks what the vegetables are; if they're not busy, they'll be glad to explain.

Turn left up Clay Street and cross to the right-hand side. Pass the first street, Waverly Place, then turn right on Spofford Alley. Walk the length of Spofford, turn right, and right again on Waverly back to Clay Street. These two narrow streets give as "foreign" a feeling as any streets I have ever been on in America. It is truly like being transported into the Far East. On them you'll see herb shops, bookstores, a temple with a huge gilded Buddha (before which you may burn joss sticks), small businesses, social clubs, tourist agencies—all catering to the residents of Chinatown. Even the sounds are exotic—the strangeness of the clattering of a fortune cookie factory, the radios of the sewing factories all tuned to the Chinese radio station, the feeling that you've really been in a foreign land even though it's only a short walk from the heart of San Francisco.

Back on Grant Avenue, keep on the right side to the Trade Center. In the lobby, up a winding stairway, is a magnificent dragon. Downstairs is a kind of Chinese supermarket. It's full of imported Chinese foods and also has a wonderful selection of cooking implements and equipment. (Here you'll learn that a flour sifter doesn't necessarily have to be made of metal—it can also be made of woven bamboo and sift just as well.) Go out the ground floor door to Portsmouth Square Park, above the parking garage. This is a heavily used park with swings and slides for little kids and playing tables for grownups. Look at the board and card games the people are playing at the tables—they'll be new to you. Usually there are several older men engaged in the solitary set of exercises called "shadow boxing."

Across the bridge in the hotel is a new feature of Chinatown. At this writing, it is in the development stage, but by the time this book is published, the new Chinese Cultural Center should be in full swing. Exhibits of art are planned, and cultural events—a performing theater of Chinese operas, plays, and so on.

Return along Brenham Place to Washington Street. The older boys might want to walk down Brenham back toward Clay Street. There's a Kung Fu studio at this writing and you can watch them practice through the front window.

Back on Grant Avenue, you'll notice that the street seems to become more Chinese the closer you get to Broadway. You'll see many delicatessens. The delicatessen windows provide great window shopping; ginger ducks being prepared (in Chinese cuisine, nearly all parts of an animal are used, so don't be surprised when the butcher chops up the head and bill of the ginger duck along with the rest of the meat); fish are alive in window tanks, and there are live chickens and ducks ready to provide the freshest of foods for supper. It's an exciting stretch of sightseeing.

Turn right on Adler Place, just before you come to Broadway, for a visit to the Chinese Historical Society Museum (see Chapter 10), and you will have seen more of Chinatown than most visitors.

There are three other features of Chinatown that should be mentioned as fun and worthwhile. The first is Chinese movies. There's one on Grant, one on Jackson and one on Broadway. Chinese movies are wild events. The action is often frantic, you can't make out exactly what is happening, and the audience appears to come to socialize instead of watching what is going on. They're inexpensive and will be something you will remember the rest of your life—especially if it is a costume piece.

Dining out in Chinatown is another grand feature of the place. The food is delicious; it's hard to find a bad Chinese restaurant; and the food is generally a bargain. The secret of eating in a Chinese restaurant is seeing what your Chinese neighbors are eating, what dishes look good, and asking the waiter for that. Most restaurants serve à la carte, complete dinners, or family style—go for the family style. Don't hesitate to attempt eating with chopsticks. The waiter will show you the basic hold. It's fun for the family and not as hard as it looks—remember, even Chinese two-year-olds eat with chopsticks.

The third good thing is firecrackers. Although the

sale of firecrackers is forbidden in California (and most other places), the Chinese use firecrackers in their religious activities and their holiday festivals and so they are exempt from the law. Firecrackers are most plentiful around the Chinese New Year celebration (springtime) and the Fourth of July. To buy firecrackers, ask the Chinese boys who are standing around the street looking as though they have firecrackers to sell. San Francisco is generally lax about blowing off firecrackers (since the Chinese kids can have them, why not the other kids?), so though it's a little sneaky to buy them, it's no terrible breaking of the law. Fourth of July in San Francisco sounds something like the invasion of Normandy—or like every small town in America on the Fourth of July forty years ago. There is something about firecrackers that makes the hearts of boys glad. If you watch how they are used, they aren't all that dangerous; just dangerous enough to make them fun.

12

Japantown

MOSTLY along Post Street between Fillmore and Laguna Streets. Drive out Geary Boulevard to Webster Street and turn right. You'll see the Peace Pagoda and the white and black buildings of the Japanese Trade and Cultural Center, you can't miss it. The big building that you pass across the street is Saint Mary's Cathedral.

Nihon Machi ("Japan Town"—referred to locally as "J Town") is the heart of the Japanese community in San Francisco and should be on your list of places to see in the city. It's not as large as Chinatown—the population being smaller—but I believe that it is even more unusual in America.

It is curious that the Japanese-Americans chose to return to this neighborhood after World War II—and not only to return, but to develop this area to what it is today. There were few places in America where the Japanese were treated worse than in San Francisco.

While the Chinese, in the early days, were discriminated against because of their race and culture, the early Japanese were not treated so harshly. They were well regarded in California as hard-working, good citizens whose ties with the old country were no stronger than those of other immigrants. After World War I, though, when Japan began its economic expansion into the Pacific trade and especially with its

military expansion onto the Asian mainland, the
Japanese-Americans in California began to be eyed
with suspicion and distrust. The Hearst newspapers
were the loudest in their warnings against the Yellow Peril even in the early 1930s. Just before World
War II, *Life* magazine published FBI findings of
bombs, spy books, and sabotage equipment of the
Black Dragon Society, a Japanese nationalistic organization in California and the West Coast. Though the
membership was always tiny, the bombing of Pearl
Harbor came and the people of the West Coast, and
especially San Franciscans, went a little crazy. It was
in San Francisco that the Japanese Exclusion Act was
upheld by the federal court. American citizens of Japanese descent were given a few weeks to sell their
homes and businesses. Then these American citizens
were herded into concentration camps beyond the
Sierras. Many San Franciscans profited by the re-
moval of the Japanese-Americans. They bought the
homes and businesses cheaply.

After the war, the Japanese-American citizens returned to this neighborhood and San Francisco went
out of its way to heal the wounds of war. San Francisco adopted Osaka as its "sister city" and provided
assistance in creating this Trade and Cultural Center.
The street signs in this neighborhood are in Japanese
and English, as those in Chinatown are in Chinese
and English.

The best place to start is at the JAPANESE CULTURAL
CENTER. There are two buildings on either side of the
Peace Plaza. The one to the east is full of retail outlets
and clothing, souvenir, and handicraft shops. If someone in the family raises tropical fish, you might want
to visit the Japanese tropical fish store on the lower
level to see some outstanding, and expensive, specimens. The building to the west also has retail outlets
selling exotic things (you can buy an oyster guaranteed to contain a pearl, for example), but it's also a
trade center, the showplace for Japanese household

appliances, electronic products, and automotive and photographic equipment. One very interesting place is the Japanese cookery display put together by one of the largest food-products importers to this country. In case after case, you see traditional Japanese meals —from breakfasts, lunches, and dinners to hot and cold picnics—all shown in their traditional porcelain, lacquerware, or nesting baskets. All the food is modeled (I almost said sculptured) so realistically that you find yourself examining it to find out how they did it. With each meal is an informative description of how it's prepared and when it's served, and a history of where it began.

Before you leave the Center, have a look at the PEACE PAGODA where an eternal flame to peace has been burning since 1968. The wooden structure on the Post Street side is a drum platform. Folk drummers perform here at the several Japanese festivals and parades during the year. (See Chapter 25.)

Japantown is not as large as Chinatown, but the shops along Post Street are interesting. You'll find excellent buys in cloth and clothing. The hardware stores sell the traditional tools the Japanese use in gardening, flower arranging, bonsai dwarf-tree culture, and carpentry. Kids will see that something as common as a saw doesn't have to look like ours to cut wood. At the Japanese grocery stores and supermarkets, you'll see yet another set of vegetables seldom seen in American markets. One thing you might like to try are the Japanese instant lunches. They look like plastic cups, and feel almost empty. Pour in boiling water and wait a few minutes and you have a full meal—shrimp, eggs, and noodles in a rich, spicy broth. The clerks will show you where they're located.

Don't miss Japantown. It's fun and interesting for the whole family.

While you're at the Japanese Center, you might want to walk across Geary Boulevard and up a block

Calendar of Events

January

San Francisco *Examiner* Games—Indoor Track and Field Competitions, Cow Palace, San Francisco.

Chinese New Year Celebration, San Francisco. (The date is set by the lunar calendar, January 23, 1974; February 11, 1975.)

February

February–March Spring Opera Theater, Curran Theater, San Francisco.

Good beachcombing after winter storms.

March

Saint Patricks Day Parade.

March–April. Irish Football and Hurling, Balboa Stadium, San Francisco.

March–April Bay Area Science Fair, Academy of Sciences, Golden Gate Park, San Francisco.

San Francisco Ballet—spring season, San Francisco.

Civic Light Opera—spring season, San Francisco.

April

Golden Gloves Amateur Boxing Tournament, Civic Auditorium, San Francisco.

Cherry Blossom Festival, Japantown, San Francisco.

Annual Coin Fair, usually held in April, San Francisco.

Apple Blossom Festival, Sebastopol.

Baseball season opens—Giants at Candlestick, Oakland As at Coliseum.

Junior Grand National Livestock Exposition, Cow Palace, San Francisco.

Dollar Opera Season—around this time or early May, San Francisco.

Annual Karate Tournament, Civic Auditorium, San Francisco.

Trout and salmon season opens last Saturday in
April to November 15.
Annual Coin Show, Jack Tarr Hotel, San Fran-
cisco.

May

Rhododendrons in bloom, Golden Gate Park, San
Francisco.
Bay-to-Breakers Cross-City Foot-Race, San Fran-
cisco.
Latin America Festival, Civic Auditorium, San
Francisco.
Yachting season opens. Many regattas on the Bay.
Spring barbecue, Audubon Canyon Ranch, Stin-
son Beach, Marin County. Portuguese Chamarita
parade and free barbecue in Pescadero, San Ma-
teo County, usually six weeks after Easter.
Same thing in Half Moon Bay seven weeks
after Easter.
May–October. Good striped bass surf-fishing on all
sandy ocean beaches.

June

Annual Ox Roast, Sonoma.
Free Sunday concerts begin—through August, Sig-
mund Stern Grove, San Francisco.
Upper Grant Avenue Street Fair, San Francisco.
Sonoma–Marin County Fair.
Napa County Fair.

July

Fourth of July Celebration, Candlestick Park, San
Francisco.
Fourth of July Water Carnival, Monte Rio, Russian
River.
Municipal "Pop" concerts—Arthur Fiedler, San
Francisco.
Sonoma County Fair, Santa Rosa.
Soap Box Derby. Check with Chevrolet dealers
for details.

Enmanji Teriyaki Barbecue and Bazaar, Sebastopol.

August
Dipsea Foot Race. Mill Valley–Stinson Beach.
Ringling Brothers Circus.
Ice Follies.
Marin County Fair, San Rafael.
Gem and Mineral Society Annual Show, Hall of Flowers, Golden Gate Park, San Francisco.
Auto racing at Laguna Seca, Monterey Peninsula.

September
Renaissance Pleasure Faire, Novato, Marin County.
Annual Scottish Games, Santa Rosa Fairgrounds.
Football season opens. Raiders at Coliseum, 49crs at Candlestick.
San Francisco Opera season opens.
Northern California Numismatic Association Coin Show, Jack Tarr Hotel, San Francisco.
San Francisco Art Festival, Civic Center. San Francisco.
Annual Grape Festival, San Rafael Fairgrounds.
Marin Art Festival, Sausalito.
Monterey Jazz Festival, Monterey
Deep Pit Barbecue and Country Fair, Freestone (near Bodega), Labor Day Weekend.

October
Blessing of the Fleet, first Sunday in October.
Columbus Day Celebration, parade and festivities in North Beach.
Grand National Livestock Exposition, Cow Palace, San Francisco.
East Bay Model Engineers Society Fall Show— model railroads. (See Chapter 23.)
Pro basketball season opens, Oakland Coliseum.
Pro hockey season opens, Oakland Coliseum.
Soccer season starts (through May) at Balboa Stadium, San Francisco. Four games are scheduled for every Sunday, weather permitting.

November

Import Auto Show, Civic Auditorium and Brooks Hall, San Francisco.

San Francisco Symphony season begins (through May).

Gray whales begin migration from Arctic to Baja California. Watch for spouting from high points along the coast.

Salmon begin spawning runs up rivers and creeks after first heavy rains.

December

Cable Car Classic—invitational intercollegiate basketball, early December. Check with Chamber of Commerce or other sources listed for location. (See page 85.)

Shriner East-West Football, Candlestick Park, San Francisco.

Dickens Christmas Fair, Old Fizziwigs Warehouse, San Francisco.

Fungus Fair in California Academy of Science Golden Gate Park. Sponsored by the local Mycology Society. Mushrooms, toadstools, and fungi.

"Holiday on Ice" show is usually here in late December.

to Saint Mary's Cathedral. It's one of the newest Catholic cathedrals in America and is a beautiful building no matter what your religion. (I will speak further of churches in Chapter 16.)

13

North Beach

NORTH BEACH, like Chinatown, is a special neighborhood in San Francisco. The birthplace of the beatniks in the early 1950s and early sixties, it is San Francisco's Bohemia, Greenwich Village, and nightclub district. It is also the Italian section of town, with great delicatessens and family restaurants. Though it's not particularly for the smaller kids, eight and under, except for the restaurants, the older kids and teenagers will like it. It's centered on upper Grant Avenue, Stockton Street, and Columbus Avenue on the other side of Broadway from Chinatown.

North Beach is a great place to stroll (which is why it's not so hot for the little ones). The Italian shops and delis are very fine and upper Grant is fun. San Francisco's major art institute is nearby, so there are a lot of art students and young folk around, and the shops along upper Grant are full of their art and handicraft. There are poster stores, funky antique shops, boutiques, coffee shops, and restaurants.

There always seems to be a holiday atmosphere in North Beach—low key, but happy. A good tour is to park at the Portsmouth Square garage, walk up Kearny Street to Columbus Avenue, then up Grant Avenue to Union Street, then back down Stockton or

Columbus and back to the parking garage. You can try it with your kids. If they get bored, Chinatown, Fisherman's Wharf, and the Embarcadero aren't far away.

14

Civic Center

THERE are few cities where you can recommend the city office buildings as a good place to take the kids. San Francisco is special, though. Our CITY HALL is so grand and gaudy, all gilt and marble, statues and carvings, that it is a universal delight—kids of all ages think it's a fine place. If you're driving, park in the Civic Center garage. (Take Geary to Mason and turn right on Turk Street. Turn left on Polk and left again on McAllister.) Now, this is a place where you can marvel at sweeping marble staircases, balconies, and the towering dome (which is a few feet higher than the dome of the Capitol in Washington).

Near City Hall are also good things to see already mentioned in other chapters. The Museum of Art is across Van Ness at the corner of McAllister; the Society of California Pioneers Museum is across the street on McAllister between Polk and Van Ness; and the Government Printing Office bookstore is in the Federal Building on Golden Gate.

15

Playgrounds

THERE comes a time in the life of every traveling kid when he simply has to bust loose and run and bang around because looking out the window of the car or walking the streets that his parents tell him are interesting and viewing the views and seeing sights and staying in motels and constant movement outside himself gets to be *too much!* The beaches offered here are great places to let off steam, but have a built-in drawback in that everything is bound to get full of sand, and shoes, socks, and pants are bound to get wet as well. When the whole family is prepared to get sandy and wet, it's okay, but if a playground break is called for between one point of interest and another, wet, sandy clothing is an inconvenience.

There are three great playgrounds in San Francisco that are near tourist attractions, offer opportunities for large-muscle activity (current educational cant phrase for running wild), and don't mess up the kids too much sartorially. All three of these places are suitable for kids of all ages (and adults).

GEORGE CHRISTOPHER PLAYGROUND. Diamond Heights. Drive out Market Street as if you were going to Twin Peaks. Turn left at the first traffic light at the crest of the hill—the intersection is Burnett Avenue and Clipper Street. Get in the right lane and turn right at the first intersection which is Diamond

Heights Boulevard. Turn into the shopping-center parking lot. You'll see the playground as you come down the hill—it's near the school. Park on the right side of the lot; you can't miss it.

This must be the most imaginative playground in the city as far as great things to climb up, jump from, and slide down are concerned. It accommodates toddlers to teen-agers with its impressive playground furniture. There are a hand-over-hand parabolic arch that could come right out of an Army obstacle course and firemen's sliding poles that you have to get to by climbing up cut-off telephone poles. The shopping center with its delicatessen lets you buy a picnic on the spot. The only problem with this or any other playground is that the kids won't want to leave. All the same, you'll find that an hour or two spent here saves you much fuss later on when you go where you want to go.

CHILDREN'S PLAYGROUND. Golden Gate Park. (See Chapter 3.)

JULIUS KAHN PLAYGROUND. Spruce Street and Pacific Avenue. Drive out Geary Boulevard to Franklin Street (just past the Jack Tar Hotel) and turn right. It's one way, so keep in the left lane and turn left onto California Street. Drive out California to Spruce Street—about a mile and a half; you'll pass Fillmore and Presidio Streets (both large). When you get to the Laurel Hill shopping center, look carefully to your right for Spruce and turn right and drive to the park. If you get to the numbered avenues, you've gone a few blocks too far and should turn back.

Julius Kahn has playground equipment, tennis courts, and a large half-wilderness area with great trees to climb on and places to jump from. It lies within the walls of the Presidio of San Francisco. (For additional playgrounds in shopping areas, see Chapter 7.)

16

Churches for Kids

WHEN KIDS REACH a certain age, they become intensely interested in religion, like to find out how others worship. Also, when a family is touring a strange city of a Sunday, they are often lost as to where to go to church. San Francisco has many beautiful churches. Some rank as tourist attractions in themselves. The Saturday newspapers have a church section where you can find your own denomination, if you wish, but the following churches are extra special.

Catholic

CATHEDRAL OF SAINT MARY. Gough Street and Geary Boulvard, near Japantown. This is a magnificent addition to the city and should be visited by everyone just to see it. The exterior, when first built, drew such comments as "it looks like the dasher of an old-fashioned washing machine." Inside, though, it is a breath-catching combination of sweeping lines, superb lighting, and architectural elements that produce both awe and joy. Don't miss it.

SAINT IGNATIUS. Fulton and Parker Streets.

SAINTS PETER AND PAUL. 666 Filbert Street.

Two excellent examples of Spanish Romanesque.

Both of these huge churches are grandly built, with abundant sculpture and beautiful stained glass—a pleasure to visit.

Jewish

TEMPLE EMANU-EL. Arguello and Lake Streets.

This is the magnificent domed building you see from Twin Peaks. The temple is open to the public and the interior, rich with marble and gold, is something to see. The ark housing the Torah is a masterpiece. In the foyer is a small museum with handicraft items from Israel offered for sale. The ladies of the temple will be happy to answer any questions.

Russian Orthodox

HOLY VIRGIN CATHEDRAL of the church in exile, 6210 Geary Boulevard (Geary and Twenty-sixth Avenue). The golden onion domes and two-story mosaics on the façade are also a recent San Francisco landmark. Built by the large San Francisco colony of anti-Communist Russian émigrés, it is both a glorious church and a testament to a persecuted faith. Most Russians here came from China. The Bolsheviks chased them to China, where they settled. Then the Maoist Communists forced them to leave there and a large number settled in San Francisco. Although the worshipers are from all walks of life, many were of high rank in the tsarist nobility, military or professional and academic stratum. The interior of the cathedral is unusual to persons used to western churches. There are no seats. The Russian Orthodox stand during the services. The priests wear gorgeous robes—the interior is fascinating. A small donation is expected when you visit the church.

Protestant

GRACE CATHEDRAL. 1051 Taylor Street on Nob Hill. This is the largest Protestant church in the city and, like St. Mary's Cathedral, it is a tourist attraction in itself. A huge Gothic edifice, it is overwhelming. Most interesting are the stained-glass windows. Some are traditional, but there is a series devoted to great men of the twentieth century, and they include John Glenn, Henry Ford, Franklin D. Roosevelt, and others. There are not many cathedrals of this size in America, especially Protestant. It is special and worth a visit in itself.

San Francisco has many, many churches of all faiths and denominations. Attending services at any of them will give your kids a special experience most tourists miss.

17

Transportation

San Francisco is unique in that it has at least five forms of public transportation that kids are not likely to see in their home towns. I'm speaking of streetcars, cable cars, ferries, railroad trains, and BART (all this, with gas and electric buses and a helicopter ride thrown in for good measure!) Although San Franciscans complain about the service at times, there are few finer public transportation systems in America. For those who would rather park their cars and take the buses and streetcars to the main tourist attractions a list of what goes where can be found at the end of the chapter.

We have already covered CABLE CARS and FERRIES in Chapter 2, so there's no reason to cover the same ground.

Streetcars

One other system that is great fun for the kids is the streetcar. For those parents who rode streetcars as kids, I don't have to explain the special pleasure of that kind of travel. Streetcars are quiet when they are at the loading area; then, when they get rolling, there is a special rumble and clickety-clack over the rails. The coach sways ponderously as though you were riding inside a whale. They are solid as a train, and when you get on a bouncing bus after a smooth experience like that you get the feeling that a bus is indeed a flimsy thing. Streetcar fares are 25¢—under five free— the same as buses. Have exact change—the drivers and conductors carry no money.

There are two streetcar rides that are especially nice; both involve rides through long tunnels and both go to good places. In both instances, board the street-cars on Market Street and take the cars going to your right, out toward Twin Peaks. (At Powell and Market, this would be on the Woolworth side of Market Street.)

N Judah Line. This car goes out Market Street to Duboce Avenue—the huge fortresslike building up to your right is the U.S. Mint—thence through the tunnel under Buena Vista Heights. You emerge on the fringe of the Haight-Ashbury area, then angle off to Irving Street. The complex of buildings up on the hill to your left is the University of California Medical Center. At Ninth Avenue, you'll turn left one block to Judah. This is the center of the health-food industry in the city, and you are a block away from one of the main entrances to Golden Gate Park. The Arboretum is just inside the gate; the Music Concourse is another short block away. The streetcar travels Judah Street through the north end of the Sunset District all the way to Ocean Beach. You are always two blocks from Golden Gate Park and the line ends at the beach. It's about a mile from the end of the line here to the Cliff House along the beach. If you wish, you can walk there and take the No. 2 Clement bus back to town. L Taraval–Zoo. This streetcar goes out Market and through a much longer tunnel beneath Twin Peaks (complete with underground stations). It trav-els through the southern edge of the Sunset District and ends up a block from the zoo, two blocks from the ocean. This is an even better streetcar ride than the Judah line, but both are very fine.

BART (Bay Area Rapid Transit)

Nearing completion, the Bay Area Rapid Transit is one of the most advanced interurban transit systems to be built in America and one that offers hope to other areas suffering from traffic, smog, and congestion problems. This is a joint effort of the counties with the most heavily traveled commuter routes. Bond issues were passed and an additional one-half-cent sales tax was self-imposed to insure not only a good, workable system, but a grand system—comfortable cars, beautiful stations, and the best of materials.

At this writing, the BART trans-bay tunnel is not yet open, but you may ride as far from San Francisco as Daly City on BART. Try to board the head car where the controls are and look through the glass door to where the driver's sitting. The controls make you think you're on a rocket ship—lights flashing, computer numbers clicking around on little screens. The acceleration is remarkably smooth and unless you look through the driver's window, you don't *feel* that you have gone from zero to sixty miles an hour in the short time you've been rolling. Even when you look at the electronic speedometer, you don't quite believe it until you look out the window and see that you're tearing along like crazy.

The closest BART station to Union Square is at Powell and Market.

Railroads

A train ride was a common experience for kids only twenty-five years ago. Airplanes and airlines are a recent phenomenon. Until some time after World War II, long trips were made by rail—the airplanes were small and their schedules were spotty. Only the very largest cities had airports that could offer nonstop flights between heavily traveled points. Now, it's the other way around and passenger trains are almost gone in America and it's hard to get anywhere except by plane. In San Francisco, though, you can take a train ride just to see how it was in the "olden days."

The Southern Pacific depot is at Third and Townsend Streets. To get there from Union Square, drive down Stockton and cross Market to Fourth Street. Drive out Fourth to Townsend and turn left a block to the depot. Public parking is in the vicinity.

The trains are diesel commuter trains. They leave about once every hour on weekdays, once every two hours on weekends—check the ticket office for times. A nice ride is the round trip to San Jose, or a shorter round trip to San Mateo. The fare at this writing is rather expensive, about $2.20 round trip to San Mateo —a journey of about twenty-five minutes each way. It's a good trip, though, through railroad tunnels and switching yards.

How to Get There By Public Transportation

Sometimes, especially in the heart of the tourist season, it's faster and less grating on the nerves to visit the tourist attractions by public transportation than to drive. As we mentioned earlier, parking can be murder. The following is a selection of buses, streetcars, and cable cars that will take you where you want to go. The telephone book, in the Yellow Pages, has a complete map of the Muni railroad routes.

First, though, there are some places that are not served by the Muni; you'll *have* to drive. They are: Twin Peaks, the Golden Gate Bridge, Fort Point, the Palace of the Legion of Honor, Josephine Randall Junior Museum, and the Embarcadero south of Third Street. Plan to use your cars for these, since the Public Transportation doesn't go there or is too complicated, involving transfers.

CABLE CARS. See Chapter 2. Board at Powell and Geary Streets.

POWELL STREET LINE. Ends at the east end of Fisherman's Wharf.

HYDE STREET LINE. Ends at the east end of Fisherman's Wharf.

STREETCARS. See beginning of this chapter. Board at Powell and Market Streets.

Buses

If you have only a short time in town, the several guided-tour buses near Union Square might be a good means of catching the highlights of the city in the fastest possible way. The only problem with tours is that kids sometimes tend to get antsy about halfway through. The following public bus lines will also take you there.

No. 30 STOCKTON. To board, walk up Stockton Street to Sutter Street. It's a handy bus that takes you to: Chinatown—get off at Clay or Washington Street after you go through the tunnel and walk down a block; North Beach–Coit Tower–get off at Union Street. The Coit Tower bus is on the corner, the most Italian section of North Beach is right around you— Grant Avenue is across the street and up two blocks; Ghirardelli Square–Aquatic Park—Get off at Larkin, Polk, or Van Ness; Union Street is four blocks up from Fillmore; Palace of Fine Arts–Exploratorium— Get off at Beach and Broderick Streets, and you'll see it to your left; Marina–Yacht Harbor—Get off at Broderick and Jefferson Streets and walk to the Bay.

No. 2 CLEMENT. Board at Stockton and Sutter Streets. It goes along Clement Street, a very interesting neighborhood, and ends at Point Lobos, which is only a short walk from the Cliff House, Seal Rocks, and Ocean Beach.

No. 38 GEARY. Board at Geary and Powell. It passes

St. Mary's Cathedral, Japantown, Cathedral of the
Virgin Mary at Twenty-fifth Avenue, and ends at
Ocean Beach.

No. 5 McALLISTER. Board on Market Street on the
Woolworth's side. It goes to the Civic Center; get off
at McAllister and Polk. Near here are the Government
Printing Office bookstore, the Museum of Art, and the
Society of California Pioneers Museum. This bus travels the whole length of Golden Gate Park. The Conservatory–Children's Playground is at Arguello; the
Music Concourse is at Tenth Avenue. Spreckels Lake
and Buffalo Paddock are at Thirty-fifth; the archery
field at Forty-eighth. Most of these features are in the
middle of the park, so you'll have about a city block's
walk from the stops I've designated. Ends at Ocean
Beach.

Going the other way on Market Street: Board any of
the buses on the Emporium side that are labeled
FERRY. They'll take you to the Financial District at
Montgomery Street; the Vaillancourt Fountain; the
Ferry Building; Hyatt House; Sausalito and Tiburon
ferries at the end of the line.

The good thing about these public transportation
lines is that they not only take you where you're going
but get you into the heart of San Francisco neighborhoods for a good look at the real city. They are also
cheap and quick, and their schedules are such that
you shouldn't have to wait more than ten or fifteen
minutes for any of them. Again, the standard bus and
streetcar fare is 25¢. Have the exact change ready
because the drivers carry no money.

18

Coming Attractions

THERE ARE AT LEAST three grand things in the works that promise children's delight. They all should be beginning in the summer of 1974; no dates or real details are possible at this writing, but here are the outlines.

In England, an exact replica of Sir Frances Drake's *The Golden Hind* was constructed in 1973. It is to sail to the Bay area in the spring of 1974 and be on permanent display at Fisherman's Wharf after it arrives. I saw a report of the exquisite detail involved in the reconstruction, and it sounds like an exciting project.

A promenade is being planned that will extend around the northern perimeter of the city from Aquatic Park to Fort Point. Much of the land covered is more or less off limits now, being in either Fort Mason or the Presidio. This should certainly provide dramatic views and wonderful places for photography.

It will probably be easier to make reservations for the tours of Alcatraz by the summer of 1974. This is the first time the island has ever been open to the public even on a limited basis, and at this writing it is virtually impossible to secure passage. (See page 33.)

It is also hoped that the entire BART system will be completed in 1974. Look for details of these events in the pink section of the Sunday *Examiner-Chronicle*.

19

Nature

THERE IS PROBABLY no other great metropolitan area in the world that offers such an astounding range of unique natural phenomena immediately at hand as does the San Francisco Bay region. In the course of a single day one can examine (and walk across) an active earthquake fault; beachcomb and search for fossils; observe wild sea mammals from a few hundred yards away; fish for crabs, trout, sea bass, shark, or flounder; gather jade, jasper, and carnelian pebbles merely by bending down and picking them up; and marvel at two-thousand-year-old redwoods. One may also pan for gold and go clamming, bird watching, rock climbing, sailing, surfing, skin diving, tidepooling, surf fishing, and rock hounding. All this may be done within the city limits of San Francisco or within twenty miles from it.

That's an amazing assortment of activities, but it's a peculiar region. San Francisco Bay is a drowned river valley within a coastal mountain range in an active fault zone. The rise from sea level to the three- and four-thousand-foot peaks of Mount Tamalpias and Mount Diablo is abrupt, so the landscape is very scenic. Some of the heaviest year-round ocean swells, on any world coastline, pound on this Northern California stretch of coast from Santa Cruz to the Oregon border—making for wildly rugged, ocean-carved beach areas. The San Andreas Fault has created lakes on the San Francisco peninsula, as well as the estuary of Tomales Bay. San Francisco Bay is salt at the Golden Gate, brackish in the north and south sub-bays, and fresh water in the immense delta region where the Sacramento and San Joaquin rivers flow into it. This provides an incredible habitat range for ocean, marsh, and freshwater fish, fowl and vegetation, and the glory of the region is the accessibility of it all. The Los Angeles area is also full of wonderful variety, but most people can't get to the best places because, in a large part, they are built upon or fenced off as private property. Here, there is a lot still available to those who want to look. It's a wonderful place for kids.

Since the ocean is the most interesting feature of the Bay region, we'll look at it first. The possibilities our coastline offers have already been mentioned, but any outing to the ocean should be approached with some planning. The tides determine what you will be able to see, what fish you are likely to catch—even where you are able to go. Much disappointment can be avoided with these simple instructions on how to read the tide table. Agate Beach in Bolinas is a magnificent place for rock hunting, tidepooling, and beachcombing. If you go at the wrong time, though, you'll find nothing but raging surf—not even a beach to walk on. In both San Francisco papers, in the weather section, you'll see a "Sun, Moon, Tides" box. The example taken from the *Chronicle* for February 2, 1973, looks like this:

TIME AND HEIGHTS OF TIDES AT GOLDEN GATE

	LOW		HIGH		LOW		HIGH	
2	04:15	2.7	10:32	5.9	17:15	−0.6	....	
	HIGH		LOW		HIGH		LOW	
3	00:15	4.9	04:54	2.4	11:07	5.8	17:06	−0.5
4	00:44	5.0	05:42	2.2	11:44	5.6	18:15	−0.3

Tide time is given in military hours, 1–24. One AM
is 01:00; 12 noon is 12:00; 13:00 is one PM, and 24:00
is midnight. The number to the far left is the date
(the papers usually give the tides for the next six or
seven days.) The number after the time is the height
of the tide above or below mean sea level. In San
Francisco, the mean sea level is measured at 3 feet
(not one foot as you would suppose). So when you
read the tide heights for February 2, you see that the
low-water level at 4:15 AM was only .3 feet below
mean sea level (which is not very low). At 10:32 in
the morning, the tide had risen almost 3 feet above sea
level, which is pretty high; then at 17:15 (5:15 PM)
the water level was more than 3½ feet below mean sea
level, which is pretty low. Along our coastline, this
means that perhaps a hundred to a hundred and fifty
feet of beach was uncovered, which usually never
sees the light of day (or clammers or tidepoolers). It
may sound complicated, but it isn't. Look at the
paper. Anything below 3 means good hunting; anything with a minus number means great hunting. The
tide times given are the times of the lowest or highest
water, and the tides are leisurely phenomena. They
come and go slowly along this coastline. The farther
out to sea you are, the sooner they come, allowing for
the curve of the coastline. The Monterey Bay Area
feels the effects of the tides about an hour earlier than
does Ocean Beach in San Francisco; Bolinas about a
half-hour earlier. Sacramento feels the effect about
seven hours after the tide at the Golden Gate Bridge.
It takes about an hour on either side of the low- or
high-water time for the ocean to adjust itself to the
tidal pull, which means you have about two hours of
prime low water time before the water will begin to
push you back. Let us see how that effects your planning. You want to go to Tomales Bay, a-clamming after
the rock cockles, and the low tide is noon. It
takes about an hour to get there and another twenty
minutes to walk to your favorite spot. This means

that you'll want to leave the city about 9:30 to take full advantage of the low tide and have two hours clamming time.

A knowledge of how to read the tide tables is of great importance, and also is a very fine thing to know in itself. If you live in the Midwest, you'll probably be the only one in town who knows how to read the tide table. That out of the way, let's examine the details.

Fishing

I'm beginning with fishing because most people like to fish and kids especially like to fish. Kids like to fish because it is one of the very few sports where, in general, they can compete with adults—all adults, on a one-to-one basis. With a little luck, the youngster can land the biggest fish of the whole party and heap glory upon himself. Fishing is a magic sport. And to visiting fishermen, the San Francisco Bay area is paradise indeed. The only problem with fishermen who have never seen the ocean, let alone fished it, is that they are surrounded with possibility but don't quite know what to do. It is hoped that this chapter will be of some help.

Salt-water fishing falls into some nine categories here: surf fishing, pier fishing, poke-pole fishing, net fishing in the surf, clamming, crabbing, mussel and periwinkle collecting, skin diving for abalone, and deep-sea fishing from party boats. The ocean and Bay waters teem with fish and the sea lions are your first clues. The sea lions who visit Seal Rocks off the Cliff House six months of the year have not come to San Francisco for a vacation. They are fish-eaters and if stripers, surf perch, and other fish weren't plentiful, they couldn't loaf and *hronk* and bite each other on Seal Rocks. One walk down any of the public fishing piers shows that "Boy, they're in there!" As you'll see later, even the fresh-water fishing is exceptional.

Salt-water fishing doesn't stick a kid in one place. We'll look at the esoterics of salt-water fishing because it's the most unusual and exciting, then go from there.

One important note. Fishing licenses are required of all fishermen over sixteen years of age, no matter whether you're fishing for sea bass or crawdads (crayfish) or clams. There's one pleasant exception—fishing from the public piers is unrestricted as to license, size, or catch. In 1974 the license for nonresident fishermen is $15, with a special $5 ten-day nonresident license. Resident or not, special stamps are required for sport-fishing the inland waters, and there is a special restriction on nonresidents under sixteen who are fishing for trout—they must be accompanied by an adult with a license and trout stamp. The fish and game wardens are numerous and carry measuring tapes. If you fish, get a copy of the sport-fishing regulations (the same place you get your bait) and follow them exactly; the fines are stiff. Now, how to fish the ocean.

Surf Fishing

To the inlander who has seen surf fishing only in *Field and Stream,* or on TV, the first impression of the surf fisherman is something like a rabbit hunter's first look at someone going after moose. The fishing rod is eight or nine feet long and *heavy*—a two-handed pole. The sinker can weigh as much as most of the fish you catch at home. The fisherman is usually encased in waders up to his armpits, and, when he casts, the bait zooms out a hundred feet or more. Of course, they're fishing for "stripers," striped bass, and the prey justifies the equipment. The minimum keeper length for striped bass is sixteen inches and the fish can weigh up to twenty-five or thirty pounds. (This is not anything particularly unusual; the minimum keeper

size for sturgeon is *forty inches!* For the visiting fisherman, it's an experience and a half, even though you
don't catch anything. Surf fishing is cold, wet work,
so bundle up. If you want to try it, surf-fishing poles
and gear can be rented at DAVE SULLIVAN'S SPORT
SHOP on Geary Boulevard around Eighteenth Avenue (no special plug—I don't know of any other
place in town that rents poles). Ask them about bait.

Stripers run through the summer and early fall. Any
of the broad sandy beaches from Stinson down to
Santa Cruz are good fishing grounds.

Crabbing

The best way to go crabbing is to first make your
own crab net. Every library in the land has in its
reference section a book called the *Encyclopedia of
Knots.* Learning to tie the basic netting knot is a matter
of about fifteen minutes. It's the most satisfying
knowledge you can gain in such a short time that I
can think of. Learning the basic netting procedure—
it's a simple matter of tying a new square to one
you've already made—gives you a really grand feeling of self-reliance. If you are ever cast away upon a
desert island, you'll know how to make a fish net and
feed yourself. With this same procedure, you can net
yourself a sixty-dollar hammock for the price of the
nylon cording.

Crab nets are merely one big hoop, about three feet
across—used concrete-reinforcing iron bent in a circle
and tied is the cheapest—with a smaller foot-and-a-
half hoop beneath, joined with netting to make a
foot-and-a-half or two-foot fetch (depth) so the crab
can't scramble out when you pull up the net. The bottom hoop is covered with chicken wire and a bait cage
of chicken wire is tied to it.

The best places to fish for crabs are the PUBLIC
FISHING PIERS AT SANTA CRUZ, PRINCETON, AQUATIC
PARK, BERKELEY, or OAKLAND. Crab fishing is especial-
ly nice for smaller kids because you can throw in the

net and look at other things until it's time to pull it up and check if you've caught anything. For those who want to fish for crabs *now*, the bait and tackle shops near each of these piers sell ready-made crab nets of several types, usually from about six to ten dollars. The bait generally used is frozen mackerel or anchovies, fish heads, or other offal—crabs like it all. Whether or not to *eat* crab caught within the Bay is a point of debate among San Franciscans, but ocean crabs, so far, are thought to be okay.

Pier Fishing

For the tourist with kids, pier fishing in the Bay Area is glorious sport. There are no licenses to buy, for one thing, but some limit on catch or size; and when you're fishing, there's no telling what you'll catch. If you haven't brought any fishing tackle along, the shops near the piers or on them sell everything. Don't bother with a pole; hand lines often catch as much as expensive rigs (*Note:* At the AQUATIC PARK MUNICIPAL PIER in San Francisco, the only bait and tackle shop around is the MUNI BAIT SHOP at Polk and North Point, at the edge of Ghirardelli Square.) You might catch a striper, a flounder, rock cod, shark, perch, ling cod, starfish, bullhead, or whatever. Public piers are found in Santa Cruz, Princeton, Aquatic Park, Ferry Building, Piers 7 and 54 in San Francisco, Berkeley Marina, Oakland Marina, and PARADISE COVE COUNTY PARK in Marin County.

Clamming, Mussels, Snails, Abalone

Clamming is one of the finest kinds of fishing kids can do; it's dirty, you get all wet, and you see all kinds of beasts in the course of your digging. There are several varieties of clams along our beaches and bays from Santa Cruz north. You might find gapers, little-necks, rock cockles, razor clams, and Washington clams. Each clam prefers a slightly different environment: open ocean; protected beach or bay; sandy, rocky, or muddy bottom. If you have never clammed, it's best to go with someone who has. If that's not possible, you can watch other clammers and follow their techniques. Clammers are generally genial folk and are happy to give you basic instructions. The equipment needed is very simple—a garden spade, garden fork, or three-tined cultivator cut down to two and a half feet. Any of these a license, and a bucket or gunny sack to carry your clams are all you need. Choose the lowest tide available, so you will have the largest digging area possible. Be very careful to check the fishing laws concerning the size and limits of clams. The fish and game wardens are always at the most popular clamming sites on good tides and they check each clam with a micrometer. The fines are steep and there's no talking your way out of it.

As to where to go to dig clams within our scope, there are several excellent clamming beds. To the south of San Francisco, there is ANO NUEVO STATE PARK near Davenport. This is also a very fine tide-pooling area and one where, if you're lucky, you can hand pick abalone at a very low tide. To the north, there are BOLINAS BAY for gapers, DUXBURY REEF for cockles, and the whole perimeter of DRAKE'S BAY and TOMALES BAY for various kinds of clams. HEART'S DESIRE BEACH in TOMALES BAY STATE PARK is good for cockles. Across Tomales Bay, around MARSHALL and DILLON, there are skiffs that will take you out to the clamming grounds in the Bay itself. Bolinas Bay is also another good clamming area. Ask at the bait shop in any of these areas or at the gas stations and restaurants for specifics.

Clamming is hard, wet, dirty work, but you get more fun for nothing than from any other type of fishing I know.

Along with clams, there are three other kinds of edible mollusks available for the picking (if you can find them). Abalone is perhaps the king of mollusks—it's flesh being regarded as superior to all others. Read carefully the regulations concerning the taking of them, the sizes, and the bag limits. Again, if you've never seen them hunted, it's well to follow someone who's doing it so to be able to recognize the beast. Because they're rare, they're not usually eaten inland. The same is true of mussels and turban snails. Both are consumed in huge numbers by other seacoast peoples, but not generally by Americans.

Mussels are common along the coast and in the bays wherever there are rocks; turban snails are found wherever shallow rocky bottoms make tide pools. Be careful with mussels, though, and strictly observe any quarantine signs you see. Mussels are amazingly efficient strainers of sea water. In the summer months, when the water warms slightly, a tiny sea creature appears along the coastal waters. Each contains a tiny hint of a toxic substance closely resembling strychnine. The mussels concentrate this chemical and eating the shellfish in the quarantine months is deadly dangerous.

It's best to taste turban snails before you catch them for your table. They're for sale in the fish markets of Chinatown.

Net Fishing, Pike Poling, and Skin Diving

These are three exotic sports that require specialized equipment and seem to be limited to their own little group of aficionados, so only a short description is necessary.

At certain times of the year, mostly spring and summer, the jack smelt and surf smelt come to shore in huge numbers to lay their eggs. To catch them, one uses either an A-frame net or a two-man beach net. As a big wave comes in, the fisherman wades into the surf, sticks his net in the sand and hopes he'll have a netful of fish caught when the wave recedes.

Poke poling is called that because that is what you do. Your fishing gear is a long pole with a coat-hanger wire firmly attached, sort of a preleader, to which a stout leader and hooks are fastened. It's rather dangerous in that you are fishing the crevices in rocks and deep tide pools. You have to watch the waves, which may wash you into the water, and the tide, which may strand you. You poke the pole into these crevices and hope that a blennie or monkey-faced eel or a sea trout will bite.

Skin diving, either with Scuba gear or without, is a very popular sport and would be more popular if the water weren't so cold. Wet suits are required. You spear fish and look for abalones or spiney lobsters, which you pick up by hand. (In Scuba diving, many instructors believe it is unsafe for children under twelve years of age.)

If you live in the Bay Area, you might want to try these specialized types of fishing; if you're just visiting, you'll have an idea of what you're seeing when you come across this activity in your wanderings.

Party Boats

If you're a real fishing family who has never fished the ocean, you might want to budget for the expense of deep-sea fishing from a party boat. These boats run from about $15 to $20 a person; they leave about 5:30 in the morning and get back about 3 PM. There is, of course, no guarantee that you're going to get a fish, but most do and the fish can be whoppers. Striped bass run to fifty pounds, as do salmon when they're running. You go beyond the Golden Gate Bridge into the ocean, where it is cold and windy and the water is usually rough. The thrill of getting a big one, though, makes the work of fishing worth it all. In San Francisco, there are two centers for party fishing boats—the MUNI BAIT SHOP at Polk and North Point (near Ghirardelli Square), and 300 Jefferson. Both of these places book trips on a number of party boats—inquire at either place for details. Kids should be over eight or nine. It's a long day, and once you're out, there's no getting off.

Fresh Water Fishing

San Francisco's LAKE MERCED is one of the finest urban fresh-water fishing spots I know of. The lake is regularly stocked with rainbow trout and, in spite of the heavy fishing, some always manage to get away and grow to monster size. You need a fishing license, with a trout stamp, and there is also a small day use charge (used to pay for the fish stocking). Boats are available for rent and it can make a grand outing even for little kids. There is usually some action, so the kids won't get bored. Russian River in the north and the delta waters from Stockton to the Bay are also excellent fresh-water fishing spots.

One very important sport-fishing regulation to remember is the fact that it's unlawful to litter within 150 feet of the high-water mark of any waters of the state.

The state Fish and Game people provide excellent ocean-fishing maps of the coastline, showing where to surf fish, go clamming, and do all other types of ocean fishing. Write to the Department of Fish and Game, 722 Capitol Mall, Sacramento, California, 95814, for the maps from Monterey County to Sonoma (there are two for this area).

Gold Panning in San Francisco

Nearly everybody who comes to California has an itch to pan for gold, and you have an opportunity in San Francisco. The beach at the end of Sloat Boulevard, by the zoo, is the most promising spot in that you're sure that there's really gold there. In the Depression, many folks set up sluice boxes and a *reported* twelve-thousand dollars was taken out of this area in three years (there probably was as much unreported). The gold lies in the black sands that you'll see in layers above the beach. The sand shifts with each storm and the spring of the year is the best time to get a good shot at it, but it can be tried any time.

Panning for gold is no great mystery, but involves a lot of work. Any shallow pan is suitable. Pile up the black sand in the pan and fill the pan full of water. Stir it up thoroughly with your fingers so that the heavy gold settles to the bottom. Slosh out the lighter sand a little at a time, stirring between sloshes, until you get the heaviest residue in the bottom of the pan —then look carefully. Anything that looks like gold *is* gold. Pick or scrape away the little flour specks, save them, and start again. Finding gold is a little like catching a fish. It is tedious and hard work, but once you get a fish or a little gold, you feel very rewarded and can brag about it forever. Any pan can be used; even a plastic dog's drinking dish can do the trick.

For those who would like to go deeper into panning for gold, the Geology Museum at the Ferry Building has a "Gold Pack" that gives the location of placer mining areas in the whole state, as well as information on how to build your own sluice boxes. It's cheap and interesting.

You shouldn't miss an opportunity to pan for gold, even if you don't find any. You can always tell about your adventure when you get back home, and with a little bit of luck . . .

Whales

The California gray whale migrates from the Arctic to its breeding grounds in Baja California within eye-sight of the coastline. The whales pass here from November to February and return again in April. Any of the high promontories along Highway 1 are good lookout points—bring binoculars. The lighthouse area of Point Reyes National Seashore, the cliffs around Pacifica, and the heights farther down near

DAVENPORT are the best watching places. Keep your eyes peeled for a plume of steam (the whale's blowing), and watch for the roll of an animal the size of a Greyhound bus. This is one of the few inhabited coastlines in the world where whale spotting is possible.

Salmon

Mostly in December and January, but any time after the first heavy fall rains, the salmon return from their life in the sea, seeking the small streams where they were born, to spawn and die. It's an interesting and somewhat sad spectacle to see the frantic fish pushing their way to death-rebirth. North and south of the Golden Gate, the best places to see the run (and in the smaller creeklets, even to touch the fish) are on MUIR BEACH–MUIR WOODS, the PAPERMILL CREEK in SAMUEL P. TAYLOR STATE PARK and the OLEMA BRIDGE in Marin County; along the SAN GREGORIO CREEK, PESCADERO area on the Peninsula. It's an outing you will never forget.

Butterflies

The butterfly trees of PACIFIC GROVE in MONTEREY are the most publicized of the "butterfly trees," wintering places for the monarch butterfly. That city has parades to the monarch and city ordinances protecting this curious insect. The monarch feeds on milkweed plants in the Sierra. Every year, masses of butterflies arrive to winter on specific trees, returning to the Sierra in the spring to lay their eggs. When mature, the baby butterflies fly to the same trees where their parents wintered the year before. It's not widely known that there are several butterfly wintering places other than Pacific Grove. The large pine and eucalyptus trees of Bolinas and Muir Beach are also refuges. The butterflies arrive around November and are sometimes difficult to see—they look like dead brown leaves and do not fly unless the temperature is above 50 degrees. But if you are lucky, you may be there at a magic moment when the sun comes out, warming the air suddenly, and these drooping butterflies detach themselves from the trees and whirl high in the clearing in a brilliant black and orange dance. The migration instinct is difficult enough to explain in huge, intelligent beasts such as whales; harder to understand in relatively simple creatures such as birds; but really impossible to figure out when it is exhibited in no-brained animals such as butterflies.

Indian Relics

The Pacific Coast had one of the largest populations of Indians on the North American continent. The lush plant, animal, and sea life supported large numbers of people so easily that they never had to develop beyond the hunting-gathering level of civilization (no agriculture, no animal domestication beyond the dog). There used to be huge shell mounds and kitchen middens to testify to the long habitation and constant use of what nature offered. Most of these village sites have long been paved over or reserved to professional archaeologists. One Indian site, though, is open to public exploration. This is at Ano Nuevo State Reserve near Davenport on the peninsula. Site of so many fine natural things (clamming, tidepooling, observing large sea mammals), Ano Nuevo's extensive middens can be combed by anyone. This is not quite so easy as it might sound. The artifact area covers the top of the bluff overlooking the oceans and is a place of high, shifting sand dunes. Finding an exposed shell mound is a matter of luck—but then, the searching is always as much an adventure as the finding.

Fossils

Fossil hunting provides fantastic souvenirs. There is something thrilling about holding in your hand the fossilized remains of an animal that lived twenty million years ago, that leads directly to the library for answers to how these animals lived, what they looked like, and how they became stone.

Although there are many fossil sites in the Bay area, the best one for kids is the stretch of Ocean Beach that runs from the zoo in San Francisco to MUSSEL ROCK down the coast on the other side of THORNTON BEACH STATE PARK. It's best because you're bound to find something, at least fossilized shells and sand dollars. Some people have found extinct camel bones and whale teeth. Start either at the parking area at the end of Sloat Boulevard or at Thornton Beach just across the county line on Highway 1.

Rocks and Minerals

Because of the active earthquake faulting, the recent mountain building, and the many raisings and lowerings of the coastline, the geology of the Bay area is fascinating, and the collectible rocks and minerals form an extremely wide range. The Napa River has obsidian and mineral specimens washed down from the dormant volcano of Saint Helena; nearby are petrified logs buried in ancient eruptions; jasper and agate pebbles can be picked up along the coastline from Russian River south (with jade and carnelian in local spots); and no limit to sedimentary and metamorphic rocks in between. The serious rock-hounding family will have already gone to the Geology Museum at the Ferry Building for books and maps detailing the Bay area geology and possibilities. The following are the best places to look for rocks, because the rocks are pretty and semiprecious stones.

Large, smooth beach pebbles of jasper, agate, and chert are found on Ocean Beach and south to Mussel Rock. These pebbles can be cut and polished, or tumbled to a high shine. FORT CRONKHITE BEACH, across the Golden Gate Bridge, has beautiful tiny pebbles of various shades of green nephrite (American jade), jasper, and gem-quality carnelian. Agate Beach in Bolinas has several unusual types of agate pebbles that are weathering out of the beach deposits. One kind is clear, light amber colored with inclusion; the other is black with lighter striations. Both are already wave-polished and can be further polished for use in jewelry. On the wild beaches near Jenner, just south of Russian River, are many wave-polished quarter- and half-dollar-sized jasper and agate pebbles of beautiful coloration. Although there are more good spots, which will be mentioned when we come to details, these are the best rock spots for kids.

Tidepools

Another wonderful family outing is a visit to one of the many tidepool areas along the coast. Again, check the tide tables for a low-tide time—a minus tide is the best. There are many, many amazing things to be seen along this stretch of coastline; eels, octopus (if you're lucky), sea anemones, sea urchins, starfish, hermit crabs, snails, and more. Some of the animals are very small, so a magnifying glass is a good thing to have along.

Be sure to take a camera along so you can photograph your kids with their finds, because that's all you're permitted to take from the tidepools you visit. Tidepools are fragile things, full of small sea life that seeks shelter there in its early growth or has developed, over the millions of years, to tolerate the higher water temperatures, lower oxygen content, and higher salinity than in the open ocean—larger creatures can't eat them there, so they survive. No "collecting" is permitted under the state fish and game laws, unless special permission is obtained.

When there was no restriction on what could be taken, there was wholesale destruction of the small creatures and some tidepool areas were stripped of whole classes of animals. Most of these animals were thrown away the next day because they died and the beautiful colors they had when they were alive faded to clam gray. They're wild creatures and live a precarious life—at any moment they may be eaten by a bird or fish, or get bounced out onto a dry place by a fluke wave and die in the sun. So don't make life harder for them than it already is. When you lift a rock to see what's beneath, do it gently, and replace it in the same way—it's some creature's home. Be patient. Most of the creatures are shy and won't come out if they see any movement above. Tidepooling is an interesting and exciting experience for all. There's more to come in future chapters.

20

South to Santa Cruz

THE SAN FRANCISCO PENINSULA is divided into three parts by the range of coastal mountains going generally down the middle, but a little closer to the ocean. The eastern, Bay part of the peninsula, once extremely beautiful farm and orchard land, is now a megapolis. The middle of the peninsula is still largely green mountains and small towns—the majority of the larger parks, including beautiful stands of redwoods, are located here. The ocean side of the peninsula is mostly agricultural, with some of the most interesting state and county beaches to be found in Northern California. The peninsula has many delightful features—so south to Santa Cruz!

There are three ways to approach it. HIGHWAY 101 travels the west side of San Francisco Bay and is simply awful. Unfortunately it is the fastest way to get to some of the points of interest, so it can't be avoided. For the whole of its fifty-mile length between San Francisco and San Jose, you get an object lesson on how man can create a fifty-mile slum highway. It was probably inevitable. The mountains forced the main railroad and highway building along this stretch of the Bay. The Bay was filled and the smaller mountains were torn down to make the fill. Factories and commerce followed the roads and railroads; cheap tract homes were built to house the workers. There was no planning, no concern for the natural beauty of the area, no control of sprawl. Vast areas of once-beautiful farm and orchard land disappeared beneath the building, so now, for the whole fifty miles to San Jose, you are never out of sight of "development." The cars and factories brought smog, so, on the sunniest days, you'll have to keep that in mind.

ROUTE 280 travels down the middle of the peninsula and is one of the most beautiful highways in the country (made so because the citizens forced the planners and builders not to repeat Highway 101). If the destination can be reached by it without too many road directions, I'll indicate it.

HIGHWAY 1 follows the ocean. It is the most scenic (glorious in spots) route south. It's also the most dangerous because it is narrow and winding and beset with pea-soup fog in some places at some times of the year. (You literally can't see twenty feet in front of the car.)

For purposes of organization, we'll go down the east side of the peninsula, explore the middle, and come up Highway 1. You can choose your own routes after you read the chapter.

From San Francisco to San Jose Along Highway 101

To reach Highway 101, drive out Geary Street to Van Ness Avenue, turn left to Eddy Street (two blocks down the hill); right on Eddy and left on Gough to the freeway entrance. Follow the signs to San Jose.

SAN FRANCISCO INTERNATIONAL AIRPORT. About twelve miles from the San Francisco city limits, you'll find the airport. It might seem odd in this day and age, when people are walking on the moon, to include an airport as a point of interest to kids, but even today it is a rare treat. This airport is especially interesting in that it is one of the major conduits of travel to the Far East. There are all kinds of people to see; planes, big and small, are taking off and landing every minute, and when you're not actually involved in the worry of getting on the right plane and seeing to your luggage, it's an exciting spectacle. If you haven't traveled on a plane recently and undergone the stringent searching procedure—*that* is an interesting experience. You don't have to be catching a plane to get searched; they search you if you're only going out to look at the planes. Kids like this especially —being taken superseriously, as if they were spies or hijackers or whatever, with a concealed submachine gun in their jackets.

One suggestion. All airport restaurants believe themselves superdeluxe caterers to gourmets—and charge outrageously for their food. Eat either before or after you go to look at the planes. There are a few stand-up snack bars if you are actually perishing with hunger and thirst.

COYOTE POINT PARK, San Mateo County. To get there: Coyote Point Park is just beyond the airport off Highway 101. Look for the San Mateo exits and take the Poplar Avenue turnoff; continue two blocks to Humboldt; turn right and continue to Peninsula Avenue; turn right again and go over the overpass to the park. The beach and rifle range are to your left on Coyote Point Drive; the marina, Junior Museum, and playground–picnic areas are to your right.

This is a fine, large county park with a great many features. There are playgrounds and picnic facilities, a swimming beach on the Bay, a pistol–rifle–range, small boat marina, restaurant, Junior Museum—in a word, a wealth of good things to do in its four hundred plus acres. The swimming area on Peninsula

Beach is especially nice, if somewhat windy, but there are scattered windbreaks for your comfort. The Bay water is warmer than the ocean water, so there is an extended swimming season here. The beach is directly beneath one of the landing patterns for the San Francisco International Airport, so you can watch the huge planes whoosh down for a landing. The pistol and rifle range is near to the beach and welcomes spectators.

MARINE WORLD. Off Highway 101 opposite Belmont (a little past Foster City). You'll see the signs. Take the Marine World Parkway turnoff.

Marine World is a commercial attraction combining ocean and jungle features. There are exhibits of sea creatures in large aquaria, sea lions, and the like, and on the boat trip you pass clusters of African wildlife. There are also almost continuous shows in the various arenas and stadia scattered through the place—dolphin shows, an extremely interesting killer-whale show, bird shows, ecology shows, a lion and tiger show, and more. Admission is expensive, but there are no other charges within the park except for food for yourselves and the sea lions—if you want to feed them—and the chance to ride on an elephant or camel. Everything else, all the various shows, is included in the entrance charge. The shows are scheduled so that something is going on every minute.

San Jose

SAN JOSE is a city you just might miss. You shouldn't. There are some good places for kids around there. Some are very fine, and some are so utterly whacky they have to be seen to be believed. All the directions given will be from Highway 101. Driving time from San Francisco to San Jose is approximately one hour. First I'll list two city parks that kids will like that will give them a chance to run and you to picnic after the drive down Highway 101.

ALUM ROCK PARK. Take the Santa Clara Street turnoff (Highway 130), which is just past the Highway 680 interchange. You'll want to drive east on Alum Rock Avenue to the park. Follow the signs.

Alum Rock Park is a large park that follows a sizable creek bed. The park is largely natural, but there *are* picnic facilities and playground equipment. The Junior Museum on the grounds has the usual compliment of small native mammals, birds, and snakes. One interesting display I've seen nowhere else is a glass cage full of black widow spiders. This park is primarily a good place to get out of your car, stretch your legs, and relax.

KELLY PARK. Senter and Keyes Streets. Take the Story Road Exit off Highway 101.

Kelly Park is San Jose's major city park, containing the zoo, children's park, Japanese Friendship Garden, and museum, as well as general park facilities. The park is relatively new and is still growing. It's highly recommended for the whole family. The hours for the various attractions in the park run generally 10 AM–5 PM in the winter months (September–June); 9 AM–8 PM in summer (mid-June–September). Variations in the hours will be given in the following descriptions.

HAPPY HOLLOW CHILDREN'S PARK. Closed January 1 through Easter. Weekends only, 10 AM–5 PM, September 11–December 31 and Easter to mid-June. Mid-June–September 10, Monday–Friday, 10 AM–5 PM; Saturday and Sunday, 11 AM–6 PM. Small admission fee.

This children's playground is on the same order as the San Francisco and Oakland children's parks. There are small rides, animals to pet, and puppet shows, as well as great things to climb on, through and over. The Paddle Boat, Tree House, Maze and Witch's House are as good as the climbables at Oakland's Fairyland, but this is a newer park and seems somewhat cleaner and more spacious than those in San Francisco and Oakland.

SAN JOSE ZOO. Open all winter, 11 AM–4:30 PM; summer, 11 AM–5:30 PM.

Although the admission price of 50¢ for adults, 25¢ for kids 5–15, seems a little steep for such a small zoo, it is really worth a visit. The animals are beautifully housed and displayed. Nearly every beast's compound is protected by a roving closed circuit TV camera that monitors the actions of the viewers to be sure the animals are not harmed. At first, this surveillance seems a little like "Big Brother Is Watching You." But having watched the unprotected animals at the San Francisco zoo fed filter-tipped cigarettes and plastic bags with popcorn inside, and deliberately teased, I think this idea is a good one.

JAPANESE FRIENDSHIP GARDEN. Down the road a little from Happy Hollow and the zoo, there is a beautifully landscaped, six-and-a-half acre, authentically landscaped Japanese garden. There is a tea house on the grounds, as well as a gift shop.

HISTORICAL MUSEUM. Monday–Friday, 10 AM–5 PM; Saturday, Sunday, and holidays, noon–5 PM. Adults 35¢; families 50¢; children 10¢.

A small museum with exhibits of local history. It shows the development of the Santa Clara Valley from Indian times to the present day. Suitable for older kids or those interested in California history.

THE ROSICRUCIAN EGYPTIAN MUSEUM, PLANETARIUM, AND SCIENCE MUSEUM. Park and Naglee Avenues.

Tuesday–Friday, 9 AM–5 PM. Saturday, Sunday, and Monday, noon–5 PM. Free.

From Highway 101, take the route 680-17 turnoff as if you were going to Santa Cruz. Take the Route 82 Alameda exit and turn left on Alameda, then right on Taylor to Park. You can't miss it. It looks as if you were in old Egypt.

The Rosicrucians are a mystical organization which, if I understand their magazine ads correctly, possesses the knowledge of the ancients and thus has acquired limitless power. San Jose is said by those who know to be a pocket of mystical vibes—one of the few such pockets on the face of the earth. This probably accounts for the fact that this organization is headquartered here.

The Egyptian Museum is a curious place. It is spooky. It has an extensive collection of Egyptian and Assyrian artifacts: mummies, statues, personal effects, combs, jewelry, and other grave objects. One fascinating thing is a life-sized reproduction of an Egyptian tomb. There are dioramas depicting day-to-day life in ancient Egypt and models of famous temples. Assyrian, Roman, and early Christian objects are also to be seen.

Adjacent to the Egyptian Museum is the ROSICRUCIAN SCIENCE MUSEUM AND PLANETARIUM. Open October–May on weekends, 1 PM–5 PM; June–September, Wednesday–Sunday, 1 PM–5 PM. There is an admission charge for the star show: adults 50¢; children under 12, 25¢. There is a monthly change in program in the Planetarium. The foyer of the building has science exhibits and may be viewed free.

WINCHESTER MYSTERY HOUSE. 525 South Winchester Boulevard. Daily, 9 AM–5 PM. Adults, $1.75; children 6-11, 50¢.

From Highway 101, take the Lawrence Expressway to Stevens Creek Boulevard. Turn left on Stevens Creek Boulevard to Winchester Boulevard and turn right.

This has to be one of the strangest dwellings in the world. It was the home of Sarah Winchester, of the Winchester Rifle fortune. When her husband died, in their uncompleted house (there were seventeen rooms at that time), she was advised by a seeress that as long as she kept building, she would never die. For thirty-six years she built, until the house had 160 rooms and rambled over six acres of ground. Secret passageways, stairs with thirteen steps, rooms with thirteen windows—it's a huge memorial to a woman's mysterious eccentricity. It's also beautiful in spots and very interesting.

FRONTIER VILLAGE Amusement Park. 4885 Monterey Road. Open in the summer, Monday–Thursday, 10 AM–5 PM; Friday and Saturday, 10 AM–10 PM; Sunday, 10 AM–6 PM. During the rest of the year, open on weekends, holidays, and school vacations, 10 AM–5 PM.

From Highway 101, drive south (it's on the south side of San Jose) to the intersection with Highway 82. Watch for the signs. It's one mile south of Capitol Expressway.

Frontier Village is a "theme"-type amusement park —in this case, the Old West. It has rides, entertainments, and attractions all revolving around cowboys and Indians. There is a shoot-out in the street every twenty minutes or so—complete with an undertaker who carries off the bad guy. There are two especially nice things for kids—a gold-panning place where the attendants teach you how to pan and find the salted gold in the gravel; and a trout-fishing pool, heavily stocked, where you're almost guaranteed a fish (you pay for it by the inch; they pack it for you to take home). The prices aren't bad for the size of the place. You can either pay admission ($2.50 each) and buy tickets for the individual rides; pay $3.25 for admission and 10 rides; or pay $3.50 for admission and unlimited rides. There are enough rides and attractions to insure that you're getting your money's worth no matter how you handle it. It's not as grand as the super amusement park in Santa Cruz, but is certainly worth visiting if you don't want to go all the way down to Monterey Bay.

To continue to Santa Cruz from San Jose, retrace to the Capitol Expressway (which turns into Hillsdale Avenue, then into Camden Avenue), and make a left turn onto Capitol. Follow it to Route 17 and turn left, then follow the Santa Cruz signs.

The Middle Route South Along Highway 280

The middle of the peninsula offers a wealth of very fine places for kids. State and county parks abound, and the country is wonderfully scenic. The middle route is also the fastest way to Santa Cruz. To go there directly from Union Square, drive out Geary to Van Ness, then turn left to Ellis or Eddy, turn right for two blocks and left on Gough to the freeway entrance. Follow the signs as if you were going to San Jose, then turn right onto the junction of Highway 280. Follow 280 to the junction of Route 17 to Santa Cruz. (It's about an hour's drive to the junction.)

The main attractions of the midpeninsula are located more seaward. Drive 280 out of San Francisco and you will pass Lower Crystal Springs Lake. This long lake (with Upper Crystal Springs Lake) lies in a valley formed by the San Andreas Fault. It is a reservoir that used to hold all of San Francisco's drinking-water supply. (The system of aqueducts and tunnels brought water from the Sierras and emptied it here, to be held until it was used by the city.) Now a by-pass brings much of the mountain water directly to San Francisco. About here, you will turn right on Route 92—the Half Moon Bay turnoff. In a few miles, you will turn left onto Route 35, Skyline Boulevard. This will take you through the heart of the peninsula and to the many parks. The country through which you will be traveling was once a great logging area—there were dense stands of coast redwood. Most of the parks that follow contain stands of these trees that escaped in the rebuilding of San Francisco.

HUDDART PARK. On Skyline Boulevard about eleven miles from the turnoff from 92. One of San Mateo County's excellent county parks, Huddart offers 970 acres of largely forest area. There are picnic facilities, playground equipment, nature trails, an archery range, and many hiking and bridle trails. Continue down 35 and turn right onto the La Honda Road. There are two more county parks within a short distance of each other.

SAM McDONALD PARK. This is between the San Gregorio Road and the Pescadero–La Honda Road in La Honda. At present, the park is under development and there are few facilities, but it is grand hiking in the four-hundred acres of undeveloped redwood country.

Continuing down the Pescadero–La Honda road is MEMORIAL PARK. Also in the redwood area, it has camping areas, nature trails, a concession stand, and swimming on Pescadero Creek.

Between Memorial Park and Portola State Park is a fifty-seven-hundred-acre county park, PESCADERO CREEK PARK. This is largely wilderness area, but with fine hiking trails. One must check in and out of this park through the Sam McDonald Park. There is no camping permitted here and no fires of any kind—that includes smoking. In the center of the park is the San Mateo County's Sheriff's Honor Camp, a detention facility. The area around it is restricted.

From La Honda, you can follow signs to PORTOLA STATE PARK. This is a developed state park with overnight camping, fishing, and nature trails in the redwoods. Some of the San Mateo County parks charge a 50¢ car-entrance fee, but most of the state parks charge a $1.00 car-entrance fee. Since the state park land constitutes some of the finest natural land to be found in the state, and the variety is almost too broad to encompass (from ocean to mountain to desert), it is a good idea for the Bay area families to buy the $10 pass. This provides unlimited accesses to all state parks for the whole year.

Now, let us return to Route 35. Passing the La Honda road, continue to the junction of Route 9 at Saratoga Gap, and turn right. Turn right again at Route 236, and you will come to BIG BASIN REDWOOD STATE PARK. (If you continued on Route 35, you would have come to CASTLE ROCK STATE PARK a few miles down the road. They are close together and should be mentioned as one. In the future, perhaps there will be public park land from Skyline Boulevard to the sea.)

Big Basin Redwood State Park is a twelve-thousand-acre preserve of virgin redwoods, a long-time popular vacation area for Bay area families. It's the oldest of California's state parks, the first eight-thousand acres having been donated to the state in 1902. It's a complete park with store and service station (in the summer months), and many miles of hiking and nature trails. This is a wonderful park for a day visit or overnight camping trips.

Castle Rock State Park, near it, is one of the newest in the California state park system, established in 1968. Its sandstone outcroppings make it a favorite of hikers and rock climbers. There is an active campaign by the Sempervirens Fund to acquire all the privately owned land still remaining between these two parks, and that from Big Basin to the sea. The Fund's address is P. O. Box 9294, Stanford, California 94305, and donations are tax exempt. As with all other scenic areas, virgin timberland, beaches, and forests, if this land is not conserved, soon, it will be built on or paved over—lost for public park land forever.

Return to Route 9, and Santa Cruz is about twenty

miles away. There is another state park between here and there, but that will be covered along with the attractions around Santa Cruz. We will return from Santa Cruz to San Francisco along the ocean.

Santa Cruz

SANTA CRUZ is a major recreation area of Northern California. It is one of the few remaining old-fashioned seaside resorts in the country, with a permanent amusement park, a boardwalk, a fishing pier, and the attendant lesser amusements and attractions usually found near any such resort. Seventy-four miles from San Francisco, it's a good two- to two-and-a-half-hour drive no matter which way you go, but it's a grand trip for the whole family.

Santa Cruz is on the northern tip of Monterey Bay in a wonderfully scenic spot. There are miles of sand beaches to the south and a ruggedly picturesque coastline stretching north, and it's only minutes from the heart of wild redwood country. The beach is one of the finest surfing beaches in the state and, since the water is a few degrees warmer than it is farther north, the beach can be used for swimming in the summer. What makes it so fine is that all the attractions are located near each other. Kids find the rides great, the beach fun, and the pier interesting. Because it is a long-time resort, there are loads of motels in and around the city, so that the price of rooms stays competitive. But let's look at what it offers.

THE AMUSEMENT PARK. The park is open all summer, of course, and with shortened hours on weekends after Labor Day. It's usually closed during the winter rainy season, reopening for weekends after around Easter. The dates are vague because parts are open all year around. It has a wealth of rides for all age groups from toddlers to grandparents, who can enjoy the scenic sky tram. The roller coasters here equal those I've seen in big amusement parks across the country—although my wife says they're not as hairy as the ones on Coney Island. Kids have died here in the last couple of years by standing up and trying other foolish bravery acts on the roller coaster, so don't fool around. With the rides, there are carnival-type skill games—shooting galleries, for example—as well as some excellent souvenir and sport-clothing shops. I enjoy the amusement park and boardwalk because it's so permanent. The pressure you feel when you go to fairs or carnivals seems to be missing, and the kids seem to feel it too. It's an exciting place, but it's not frantic.

THE SANTA CRUZ PIER. Like all public fishing piers, this offers not only good fishing but good walking around and seeing what others have caught. Santa Cruz is an excellent base for all kinds of sports fishing. Surf fishing, clam digging, pier fishing, and skin diving are all available in town or near it. There are party fishing boats leaving from the fisherman's wharf and skiffs can be rented if you want to fish away from shore. The pier and the fisherman's wharf, which has good restaurants, are enjoyed by all.

Near Santa Cruz

As you come down Route 17 to Santa Cruz, you'll see billboards advertising various amusements aimed at children and tourists. There's a Santa's Village, another Frontier Village, and so on. All are the sort of one-armed entrepreneurship that flourishes around any major amusement center. Each is one man's idea of what would be of interest and every one in its own special way is different. All charge admission, and will be only briefly described because time spent there could be better spent elsewhere.

SANTA'S VILLAGE. On Highway 17, a few miles north of Santa Cruz. (You'll pass it when you come from San Jose or Route 280.) This is an amusement park built around the Santa Claus theme. He's there all year around. There are reindeer to pet, rides to ride, puppet shows, and other amusements.

LOST WORLD. Near Santa's Village on 17 on the opposite side of the road—you can't miss it because huge Fiberglas dinosaurs will be staring at you on the freeway. This is a curious place. The dinosaurs have been put up to attract the kids, but the main feature of Lost World is an amazing exhibition of grafting by the original owner. He transformed trees into ladders, chairs, cages, spirals, and steeples, and Lord knows what. It's a rather seedy place but can be of interest to gardeners.

MYSTERY SPOT. On Branciforte Drive, about three miles north of Santa Cruz. Follow the signs. The laws of gravity are apparently defied in this curious place. The kids will be entirely mystified as to why they can't stand up straight on a seemingly level floor—and so will you, until you ask the guide. There are picnic areas and playground equipment.

There are two major attractions near Santa Cruz, located near each other by Felton, a few miles north of Santa Cruz on Highway 9.

HENRY COWELL REDWOOD STATE PARK. This seventeen-hundred-acre state park offers the whole range of park facilities: overnight camping, trailer hookups, food for sale and a restaurant, swimming, fishing hiking, and horse-back-riding trails. It's a fine stand of virgin redwood forest (one tree here is over 250 feet tall), and is centrally located for camping out only a short drive from the amusement centers of Santa Cruz and the ocean.

Roaring Camp and Big Trees Narrow-Gauge Railroad. Take Highway 9 to Felton and turn right back to Graham Hill Road. It's across the railroad tracks from the concession area of Henry Cowell Redwood State Park.

This is one of the best attractions around Santa Cruz. It centers on an 1890s narrow-gauge logging railroad that takes you for an hour's ride up into the mountains and back again. The price at this writing is around $3.50 for adults and about half that for kids. The ride through the stands of timber, up the mountain over crazy trestles, is a joy—as is the chuff-chuff of the specially built steam locomotive. All the rolling stock is the original, used almost a hundred years ago. In the middle of the trip, on top of the mountain, the train stops for a rest at a picnic grounds and you may stop off here and catch a later train back (they run every hour in the summer). At the boarding area is an old general store (selling old-fashioned candies, posters, souvenirs, and antiques), and an antique ticket office and caboose made into a snack stand. There is a stocked trout-fishing pond nearby and, while waiting for the train, you can walk across the railroad tracks to the state park for a walk to the redwood grove, which is nearby.

From Santa Cruz to San Francisco Along Highway 1

Highways 101 and 280 are very quick—you can travel the whole seventy-six miles to Santa Cruz or back in an hour and a half or two hours. Highway 1 is much slower because it is two lanes most of the way, and it winds. There is a wealth of fine ocean things to see and experience along this stretch of coastline, including five county beach parks, fourteen state park beaches, and at least ten private beach-access points. Along the way are spots where you may go clamming, surf casting, rock fishing, abalone picking, tidepooling, skin diving, surf netting, as well as look for whales in their season, watch sea lions and sea elephants, hunt for rocks and fossils, dig for Indian relics, swim, beachcomb, and just plain loaf, or play in the sand. We'll list all of them for the Bay area family, and emphasize the best for the visitor whose time is limited.

The drive from Santa Cruz to Davenport is scenic but offers little access to the ocean. There's rock fishing all along this stretch and some skin diving, but the land is mainly agricultural and the steep cliffs don't offer a safe place to take kids to the ocean. There is private access to the beach at Davenport landing, Davenport Beach, and Scott Creek Beach. Davenport is a curious little town. It was a whaling station at one time—preying on the California gray whales as they went past the town in November and back again in April. From the road, you can still see the ruins of the town jail. At Greyhound Rock, there is parking on the cliffs and a trail to the beach, where you can camp or picnic, rock fish, surf net, or skin dive. Little parcels of Big Basin Redwoods State Park land around Waddell Creek extend to the sea, but one of the finest spots on the whole coastline is only a little way north.

ANO NUEVO BEACH STATE PARK. The only thing wrong with this park is lack of access. You have to park on the road and walk down to the beach, then up a steep path to the trail, which skirts an artichoke field on one side and a hundred-foot sheer cliff on the other. It's about a mile hike into the main part of the park, which is a long walk for little kids. There are so many good things about this park, though, that the work is worth it.

Around the periphery of the park is an excellent tidepool area, and good clamming grounds for rock cockles—littlenecks—the finest-tasting steamer clams found anywhere. While digging for the clams, you're apt to uncover anything, from tiny octopus to eels to starfish to sea anemones. If you go clamming, be gentle with the other invertebrates—put the rocks back where you find them. On low tides, you may find keeper-sized red abalone just by wading a little deeper. The skin diving is excellent around here.

Before leaving the trail and descending to the beach, you will see an island offshore with houses. This was an old Coast Guard station, now abandoned but not uninhabited. Take your binoculars so you can see that it has become a breeding colony for sea lions and the rare sea elephant. The island is strictly off-limits to all but the marine biologists who use this for studying these huge sea mammals. The animals have taken over the island and the houses. You can sometimes see a sea lion taking his ease on a porch of one of the houses, just like an old burgher surveying his property. From reports of the biologists, it seems that the sea lions are not at all housebroken and extremely untidy.

To get to the beach area, you walked through an extensive area of sand dunes. The richness of the sea bounty of Ano Nuevo supported many generations of Indians, who camped on these dunes, leaving vast kitchen middens of clam shells, fish bones, and their own discarded household utensils. The dunes shift in the constant wind, covering and uncovering the middens. It is permitted to search these for relics of the Indian days and with a lot of searching and a little luck, you may take back home a truly memorable souvenir.

Farther north, you'll pass the Pigeon Point lighthouse, then come to Arroyo de los Frijoles (Bean Hollow—*frijoles* is "beans" in Spanish) and Pebble Beach—both state park beaches.

A friend who writes for *Field and Stream* and *Sports Afield* says that the entrance to Bean Hollow Creek is one of the best places along the coast to watch the spawning salmon gather for their entrance into fresh water, to lay their eggs and die. He says that the best time to see this phenomenon is after the first big winter rain, then for about a month or so.

PEBBLE BEACH STATE PARK is nearby and was a resort area around the turn of the century. It's named for the wave-polished quartz and jasper pebbles that cover the beach there—originating in a quartz outcropping offshore. An early visitor was amazed to find other tourists to the resort ignoring the grandeur of the ocean and spectacular scenery, and lying on their stomachs on the beach collecting pretty stones. You'll see their modern-day counterparts doing exactly the same thing here, and at Fort Cronkhite and near Jenner, a hundred miles north. You can look at pretty scenery all along this coastline, but a pretty rock is a jewel. Pebble Beach is also a wonderful tidepool area.

PESCADERO STATE BEACH. There is surf casting here as well as rock fishing and tidepooling. Unusual for this coastline, there is swimming in the sun-warmed delta of Pescadero Creek.

POMPONIO and SAN GREGORIO STATE BEACHES. These are sandy beaches, good for surf fishing for sea bass and surf perch—and walking around, beach-combing, and building sand castles.

HALF MOON BAY. At FRANCIS BEACH, DUNES BEACH, VENICE BEACH, ROOSEVELT BEACH, and HALF MOON BAY STATE BEACH there are a whole string of oceanfront areas open to the public, with picnic facilities and good fishing. Half Moon Bay is a small fishing-farming community, quaint and charming. There are two public fishing jetties and rental skiffs as well as party fishing boats are available. Half Moon Bay is the pumpkin-growing center along this stretch of coastline and San Franciscan families have made a tradition of going down to the pumpkin farms around Halloween and selecting the pumpkins in the field for Halloween jack-o-lanterns.

PRINCETON. Just above Half Moon Bay, this is an old-time fishing village with two public fishing jetties. HAZEL'S PIER offers some of the finest fish and chips to be found in the world and the whole area from here to Moss Beach offers excellent skin diving and rock fishing.

MOSS BEACH, just above Princeton, was an excellent tidepooling area. The problem was that it was too popular. For many years, high-school biology classes were brought here to observe tidepool life— and most of the students took home samples. As a result, the invertebrate life was swept away as if a huge vacuum cleaner had swept the area, so depleting the natural fauna that the place once full of life is now almost a desert. Moss Beach and the Montera Marine Reserve a little to the north are now closed to any kind of invertebrate collecting.

MONTERA STATE PARK BEACH is just above Moss Beach and is a fine place for sandcombing and surf casting for sea bass. A little to the north is DEVILS SLIDE, a dangerous area of steep cliffs. It was the favorite dumping ground for bodies, killed during the Prohibition gang wars, and still gets its share of rock climbers and unwary fishermen attempting to negoti- ate the steep cliffs. The cliffs, though, offer a fine lookout for migrating whales.

THORNTON BEACH STATE PARK. There are a few beaches and access points to the ocean from Montera to Thornton Beach State Park, such as SAN PEDRO BEACH and SHARP PARK, but from Thornton Beach you can reach any of them with a little walking. Thorn- ton Beach State Park is just over the San Francisco

city-county line. Thornton Beach is special for two reasons. First, it is one of the few places where you can
walk over an active earthquake fault line, and a famous one at that. When you drive down Route 280,
you see the two lakes formed by the San Andreas
Fault. Here, you can walk upon the fault line itself,
seeing where it comes from the ocean and plunges
through the cliffs. Exposed through the faulting are the
cliffs of Thornton State Park to the San Francisco
city limits and beyond to the zoo. The rocks lifted
by this active fault line expose ancient bedrock that
contains million-year-old fossils, everything from fossilized sand dollars to camel bones and whale teeth.
Stop at the Ranger's Station, where you pay your $1
parking fee, and see examples of what you are looking for. Second, Thornton Beach is one of the best
beaches for surf casting for sea bass or surf perch. It
might be noted that collecting is prohibited within the
park itself, but allowed on either side of the park there
is a fine nature walk, and the high cliffs offer great
updraft for model gilder flying and hang-glider activity.

21

North to Russian River

THE COUNTRY TO THE NORTH of San Francisco, across
Golden Gate Bridge—Marin, Sonoma, Mendocino, and
Napa Counties, has always been a favorite resort area
for Bay area families. The land to the north is the
least populated of the three sections that roughly form
the Bay area. Industry, commerce, and therefore suburbs, formed around Oakland and the East Bay, and
San Francisco and the peninsula. Here were the
deep-water ports, the railheads, and access to the
wealth of the interior valleys. Marin, Sonoma, and
Napa were separated by the waters of the Bay from
the concentration of economy and population possible
in the East Bay and on the Peninsula. The nearest
towns along the Marin Peninsula—Sausalito, Mill Valley, San Rafael—were always little towns, and so re-
main—in comparison with the sprawling suburbs of
the San Francisco peninsula and the East Bay. Sausalito was a fishing village; Mill Valley was a small logging community; San Rafael was a small agricultural
village centered in the northernmost mission of those
founded by Fra Junipera Serra.

Before the Golden Gate Bridge, travel to Marin was
not especially easy—it took a passenger or auto ferry
to get there, and so the development of that area was
slower. It wasn't until the Golden Gate Bridge was
built that real suburban growth started.

The lack of wholesale development left large areas of natural, unspoiled country—ideal for recreation. There are Bay and Oceanside parks; magnificent stands of redwoods (Muir Woods is the most famous); mountain parks, and at least twenty miles of river play area.

MUIR WOODS NATIONAL MONUMENT. Take Highway 101 to the Muir Woods–Stinson Beach turnoff. If you follow the signs directly to Muir Woods, you're in for a fairly hairy drive. It's not unsafe. Sightseeing buses use this road, but it takes careful driving. An easier route is to pass the first turnoff to Muir Woods (this is after you have left 101, turned left at the red light in Tamalpais Valley, and started to wind up the hills) and continue as if you were going to Stinson Beach. In the flatlands by the creek, you'll see another sign to Muir Woods. Follow it.

Muir Woods is an intensely visited attraction for tourists, and no wonder. Only about twenty miles from San Francisco, this virgin grove of redwood giants boggles the minds of first-time visitors from the Midwest and East whose concept of a big, old tree is one four feet in diameter and two hundred years old. These trees run three times that in size and some are over two thousand years old. As you walk through this grove of giants, you understand how primitive folk could worship trees, for they command awe even today. Curiously, though they might seem slow and patient trees because of their great size and age, the coast redwoods are vigorous growers and timber companies replant them regularly in their tree farms. The reasons that they reach such age and size are the curious properties of the species. The heavy bark is highly resistant to damage by forest fire and the wood itself has a built-in resistance to wood rot and insect damage. In the gift shop, you can buy your own little redwood burl, which will sprout and grow into one of these giants in two thousand years. (It will grow into a sizable shade tree in about ten years if the weather is right.)

To the kids, especially those from toddler to pre-teen, this is a magic forest. It's all they've heard about in fairy stories—trees that have caves in them large enough to stand up in and lie down in. It's glorious to see them sort of click out of mundane reality and immerse themselves in this special unreal reality they always knew existed somewhere. It's so special with kids that most grownups immediately feel shut out even from their own children. Even for grownups, one's first experience with a giant redwood is a memorable point in one's life.

The park has a snack bar and souvenir shop. No picnicking is permitted in the park itself, but one may tailgate in the parking lot—there are receptacles for litter there. If there is time for only one thing to see outside San Francisco, Muir Woods is the place to go.

FORT CRONKHITE. Across the Golden Gate Bridge, take the second exit (the first is the viewing area) and drive down the hill. You'll turn left at the sign pointing to Fort Cronkhite. Drive through the military reservation to the parking lot between the road and the beach.

Fort Cronkhite Beach is open to the public and is to become part of the National Golden Gate Recreational Area. It has two great features to recommend itself to kids. First is the tunnel. Near the entrance, you must go through a tunnel underneath Highway 101. It's a one-lane, very dark, very long and spooky tunnel. (Pay attention to the stop lights on either side.)

The beach at Fort Cronkhite is the destination, though, and is well known to rock-hounding Bay area residents, fortunately not too well known to many others. It's an exposed beach on the Marin headlands with dangerous surf, and steep beach. This makes it unsuitable for splashing in the water but also creates perfect conditions for wave-tumbling rocks. Offshore are ledges of jasper, agate, nephrite (California jade), and carnelian. These are broken, rounded and wave-polished to beautiful pebbles of semiprecious stone that are suitable for jewelry. (With a little finish polishing, you can make them go from gleaming to shining.) The "jade" nephrite is extremely close chemically and physically to the Oriental jade—jadite. It ranges in color from the subtlest off-white green to leaf green. The jasper is in shades of brown and the carnelian is various shade of orange (they're small, about the size of a grain of rice to the size of a pea —but most are of gem quality). It's one of the few places in the world where one can pick up "jewels" from the ground and the kids instantly recognize it as a treasure spot. When they get bored, there are hills to climb and a hike down the beach to observe the sea birds of "Bird Rock." Bring your binoculars.

SAUSALITO and the SAN FRANCISCO BAY MODEL. Across the Golden Gate Bridge, turn right at the second turnoff and follow the road down into and through town. The trip down the hill (or series of hills) gives extremely fine views of the Bay on the way down to Sausalito. Sausalito was originally a small fishing village, then became something of an artist-bohemian town—which it still remains. It's a wonderful town to stroll through. There are fascinating shops and some good restaurants, and even little kids will put up with some browsing because you get a close sea- (or Bay-) level view of sailboat activity.

SAN FRANCISCO BAY MODEL. 2100 Bridgeway. (Bridgeway is the main street of Sausalito. The Bay Model is on your right, housed in an immense building with the castle of the Army Engineers on the front.) After you pass through the downtown section, look at the houses and slow down when you reach the 2000 block. The road you want is narrow and you might miss it the first time if you aren't looking for it.

It's exactly what it says, a model of San Francisco Bay. Since the Bay Area covers an area of some four-hundred square miles, you can imagine that this model is immense. It covers a floor space of several acres. The hours are Monday–Friday, 9 AM–4 PM, and there is open house on Saturday, usually the first and third Saturdays of the month. Before you go on a Saturday, call 332-3870 to see if they are open.

For any kid who has put together model planes or cars, this has to be a fantastic model. It is an exact reproduction of the Bay, sub-bays, river systems, sloughs, tidal channels, showing the various hydraulic forces operating in an immense body of water. With it, the Corps of Engineers can solve problems: for example, a developer might want to build a bayside retirement community of ten thousand units. The sewage system that he plans will discharge so many hundred thousands of gallons of secondary treated sewage into the Bay each day. Can the Bay handle it? What would be the effect of cutting a diversion channel in the San Joaquin–Sacramento River delta area to send fresh water south for irrigation? This is where these questions are answered, and the whole family will enjoy walking over the Bay from San Francisco to Sacramento in a few minutes.

Marin County Park Beaches on the Bay

All directions are from Highway 101.

PARADISE BEACH PARK. On the Tiburon Peninsula. No pets allowed. Take the Tiburon-Belvedere turnoff. For a very scenic ride, follow Tiburon Boulevard all the way around the point of the peninsula. For a short cut, turn left onto Paradise Drive at the bottom of the hill after you pass the Belveron homes area. Follow the signs.

Paradise Beach Park has wonderful views of San Pablo Bay and the San Rafael–Richmond Bridge, and a large grassy picnic area, hills to climb (watch out for the poison oak), and a relatively safe beach. The main feature of the park is a very fine public fishing pier that always seems to have a lot of action. The sandy-pebbly beach is great for toddler-splashing and real swimming by the older kids. This cove is protected, so the water temperature is usually higher than in the middle of the Bay. There is no life guard, but on sunny days there are usually enough people watching out for each other to make the swimming safe.

McNEAR'S BEACH PARK. On the San Pablo Road near San Rafael. Fee here for parking, no pets allowed. The park can be reached either by taking the Third Street off-ramp to downtown San Rafael, then turning right (toward the Bay) on San Pedro or by staying on the freeway past San Rafael and taking the Marin County Civic Center turnoff on the other side of town to San Pedro Road.

McNear's Beach is a bayside park with picnicking facilities, tennis courts, swimming pool, beachcombing, and fishing. The swimming pool is open during summer months and has a wonderful feature for kids and adults as well. At frequent intervals, the whistle blows and the kids must leave the pool to let the adults swim in peace for ten minutes or so (without worrying about running over little ones). The kids don't mind it because they feel it's fair to share—and they can bust loose when the pool is for all without getting shouted at for accidental or incidental splashing and water fights. The walk along the Bay shore is interesting, for there are good rocks to investigate as well as old clams and shellfish weathering out of ancient clay. This area was recently (geologically) raised (or the sea level has dropped) to expose the once-submerged Bay bottom. Here you can see how animals and shells begin to become fossilized.

San Rafael Parks

All directions from Highway 101.

There are two good city parks in San Rafael for kids. They are at either end of B Street. B Street is one way going down toward Albert Park and the Louise Boyd Marin Museum of Science. To get to both of them, take the downtown San Rafael turnoff and keep in the left lane so that you'll go under the freeway into the main downtown area. For Boyd Memorial Park turn right on A Street to Mission and then left a block.

BOYD MEMORIAL PARK has picnic and barbecue facilities, fine playground equipment for smaller kids, and a great hill to climb, at the top of which is a fenced-off pond where you can see turtles basking on the rocks, huge pollywogs of bullfrogs, and lots of minnows.

Boyd Park is the site of the MARIN HISTORICAL MUSEUM, a small, but interesting and nicely kept collection of Marin County artifacts and lore.

ALBERT PARK and the LOUISE A. BOYD MARIN MUSEUM OF SCIENCE. Turn down the one-way B Street to Albert Lane and left.

Albert Park is a good-sized municipal park with picnic tables, tennis courts, ball fields, lots of green grass where kids can stretch their legs, and playground equipment for toddlers. It's on the left side of Albert Lane. Go down a little bit and cross the bridge and you are at:

LOUISE A. BOYD MARIN MUSEUM OF SCIENCE. Open Tuesday–Saturday, 10 AM–5 PM. Free. This is not only a very fine junior museum–zoo, with a resident bear, badger, and eagle and several transient injured wild beasts (brought here to recover before being returned to the wild), and pettable animals and snakes inside, but it is also a nature-ecology focal point for Marin County. They have an extremely wide range of programs for everyone, preschoolers to adults, covering everything from the famous Terwilliger Trips (run by Elizabeth Terwilliger, Mother Nature of Marin County, who is famous for her excellent work with little kids); to "Indian Life Skills" for the six to eight-year-olds; to "Wild Animal Care" for older kids and adults, teaching them how to care for injured wildlife. It's a fine place for tourists to visit and an even better place for Bay area families to become involved.

MOUNT TAMALPAIS STATE PARK. Take the Muir Woods–Stinson Beach turnoff from Highway 101 to the sign pointing out the Mount Tamalpais Road.

Mount Tam rises abruptly from the ocean to its 2586-foot summit—the peak offers a spectacular view of the Bay and ocean. On a clear day from sea level, one can make out the Farallon Islands on the horizon thirty miles away. From the summit of Mount Tamalpais you can see *over* the islands. In ancient times, this mountain was revered by the local Indians because, from some spots, the outline of the mountain looks like the profile of the sleeping Indian maiden, Temelpa.

The slopes of Mount Tamalpais contain great hiking trails; unspoiled wild country (Muir Woods is on its lower slopes); lakes (reservoir for Marin County water supply); camp and picnic ground; fine rock hounding and cliff areas where rock climbers practice mountain climbing. The hiking trails are very special, with forty-seven walk-in camp grounds. This place is excellent for the out-of-doors family.

The state of California is roughly the size of Italy, about 800 miles long and 150 wide, and Highway 1, which follows the coastline from Mexico to Oregon, is one of the most spectacular highways in the world. From Santa Cruz to San Francisco, the topography has immense variety, and in this stretch of Highway 1 from the Golden Gate Bridge to Russian River it is, if anything, more varied. We find not only exposed coastline and narrow bays, but deep fault-line estuaries and more and wider rivers entering the sea. There are stretches that remind one of the Atlantic coast around Massachusetts and the wilder coastline of Devon in England. Some places look like the Chesapeake Bay area. Even without stopping, a drive straight up Highway 1, from the bridge to Russian River, would be a memorable two- to three-hour outing for the whole family. But don't do this. There is so much more to this stretch of coastline. Following are the high points of interest along the highway. There are myriad lesser ones.

Driving from the Golden Gate Bridge, we've already visited Fort Cronkhite beach and Muir Woods. If you continue straight ahead, there is a small beach where Muir Creek reaches the ocean; this is MUIR BEACH and there are good poke-pole fishing, abalone seeking, and rock fishing there, but it's rather wild, as is the stretch of coastline from the first glimpse of the ocean to the stretch of sand at STINSON BEACH STATE PARK. As you drive this corkscrew road, you can understand why the state labels this area, "Access difficult and dangerous." But it's beautiful scenery.

STINSON BEACH STATE PARK is a lovely stretch of broad sandy beach; it's a resort town in a small way. There are swimming for the hardy and beach sports for everyone. There are restaurants and snack bars as well as grocery stores and delicatessens where a picnic can be made up on the spot. After the twisting road around the mountain, it's a good spot to take a break. From here up to about Bodega Bay, the road is more or less level, through beautiful rolling farm land or near sea level along the two estuaries. You don't have to worry about mountain driving for a while.

Stinson Beach to Bolinas

Highway 1 follows the shoreline of the Bolinas Bay. At low tide you can go clamming in the mud of the lagoon for gapers and Washington clams, or surf fishing for perch and striped bass along the shore. Near the end of Bolinas Lagoon is the AUDUBON CANYON RANCH.

Bought and maintained by members of the Audubon Society, the AUDUBON CANYON RANCH, is a wildlife preserve especially noted as the nesting grounds for the great blue heron and the common egret. There are nature trails and an ecology center. Although it is generally open to the public on weekends in the spring, the hours change. When in Stinson Beach (or San Francisco), call 383-1644 before you make plans to visit.

Turn left from Highway 1 to the Olema–Bolinas Road and you will come to Bolinas.

BOLINAS was always a sleepy, charming little village of summer homes, with year-round residents engaged in fishing or agriculture. Recently it has been "discovered," especially by artists, bohemians, and hangers-on. (For a while it seemed that every major rock band owned a house and property—sometimes lots of property—in Bolinas). This meant some unwanted development by the quick-buck builders, but that seems to be subsiding now. Bolinas is still a beautiful little town to walk around in. There are good restaurants and good fishing and clamming. The greatest thing about the town for kids is the DUXBURY REEF, which extends out into the ocean and provides wonderful tidepooling. The best place is AGATE BEACH COUNTY PARK. The best way to get here is from the Olema–Bolinas Road, just after you pass the old-fashioned schoolhouse. Turn right on Mesa, then left on Overlook and right on Elm to the parking lot. This way, you'll see some of the extremely interesting, individually designed homes of the peninsula.

Be sure to check the tide tables before going to Agate Beach. If the tide is high, the beach disappears. At low tide, though, there are wonderful tidepooling (one is not permitted to take marine specimens), beachcombing, and rock hunting. There is a reef of wave-polished agates ranging in color from milky translucence to deep black that are continually washing out of an older sedimentary deposit. With a slight finishing polish, these are suitable for jewelry.

Bolinas to Tomales Bay

From Bolinas Lagoon to the end of Point Reyes at the mouth of Tomales Bay, you will be following the San Andreas Fault line. The left side of the road is creeping slowly northward in relation to the right side. At the headquarters of Point Reyes National Seashore, you'll be able to see the effects of the 1906 earthquake most dramatically. You can think of this while you drive up to Olema. You'll like this road. Beautiful, unspoiled farmland—no towns, no stores, no clutter.

SAMUEL P. TAYLOR STATE PARK. At Olema, turn right to Samuel P. Taylor State Park about six miles inland. The park can also be reached from Highway 101, if you take the Sir Francis Drake turnoff and follow the signs.

Samuel P. Taylor has always been a favorite park for San Francisco and Marin families. It's close at hand and offers full-range camping facilities in more then twenty-five hundred acres of redwoods, creeks, and wild countryside. Papermill Creek, which flows through the park, offers a fine place to watch the silver salmon and steelhead trout in their winter spawning runs. (There's also good trout fishing here in the regular season, from May to November.) Samuel P. Taylor Park is so close to the ocean attractions that many families use it as a base camp for their trips to Stinson, Bolinas, Point Reyes, Tomales Bay, and Bodega.

POINT REYES NATIONAL SEASHORE. From Highway 1, a little way out of Olema, follow the signs to the Point Reyes National Seashore Headquarters. One of America's newest national parks, Point Reyes National Seashore was established to preserve this unique stretch of scenic and historic coastline for the public. (Before 1962, when Congress authorized the purchase of sixty-four thousand acres, there was danger that the whole lot of it would be lost to private development.) The park is of considerable historic interest. Drake's Bay has been pinpointed as the place where Sir Francis Drake beached his *Golden Hinde* to make repairs in his round-the-world voyage of 1579. Here also, Captain Sebastian Rodriquez Cermeno beached his craft for repairs on a trading voyage between Mexico and the Philippines in 1595. Drake claimed the area for England, but the name given it by Don Sebastian Vizcaino in 1603 stuck and the area was always under Spanish or Mexican control until California became American. All three of these explorer-pirate-traders thought Drake's Bay was a pretty fair bay—as far as the California coast was concerned. All three of them missed San Francisco Bay, the fairest bay of all, because of dense fogs at the Golden Gate.

At the park headquarters near Olema, you'll find all the information you need about hiking and bridle trails, the high points of each section, and a display of some of the flora and fauna to be seen here. Two fascinating things are within walking distance of the park headquarters.

The first is a working blacksmith shop. Here you can see an artisan forming hinges, boot jacks, candlesticks, and horseshoes just as all blacksmiths have done since the discovery of iron. The second item of interest is the earthquake walk. Right here was the location of the 1906 quake's rise from the sea, when it wrenched the whole coastline from here to (and past) San Francisco. You can see the offset fences, roads, and creeks and the effects of what happens when one side of the fault line stays still and the other side moves fifteen feet or so all of a sudden.

From the park headquarters, there is a new road to Limantour Estuary on Drake's Bay. Formerly this was a hiking trip along a private road. Limantour Beach is a wonderful wide, safe, sandy beach, great for exploring, beachcombing (good sea shells) and surf fishing. To get to the other side of Drake's Estuary and other features, return to Sir Francis Drake Highway and continue through Inverness.

INVERNESS is a small summer resort and fishing village, the only town on the west side of Tomales Bay. This end of Tomales is low, remote, and dramatically affected by the tides. Because of the scenery, the availability of all kinds of recreational facilities close at hand, and the fine restaurants in town, Inverness is a magnet for fishermen, vacationing families—and honeymooners. Skiff rentals are available, and there are grocery stores where picnics can be bought in preparation for the attractions farther along Sir Francis Drake Highway.

TOMALES BAY STATE PARK. After you leave Inverness, the road ascends into the hills, then divides. The road to the left will take you to Drake's Beach in Point Reyes National Seashore, while the right will take you to Tomales Bay State Park and farther on out to McClure's Beach and Tomales Point.

The main road into Tomales Bay State Park is labeled "Heart's Desire Beach." There is the usual one-dollar fee for parking, but it is worth any kind of fee. The road down to Tomales Bay gives you access to INDIAN BEACH, HEART'S DESIRE BEACH, PEBBLE, SHALLOW, and SHELL BEACHES. At Heart's Desire, there is a roped-off swimming area on the Bay (the water is very comfortable here any time the sun is shining) and picnic areas that are unique, in that each table or group of tables is separated from the others so you almost seem alone in the woods. There is great littleneck clamming to the north and south, and at low tide there are sea caves to explore. This was Indian country, so look for Indian relics.

McCLURE'S BEACH–TOMALES POINT. Continuing out Pierce Point Road past Tomales Bay State Park, you reach McClure's Beach. This is a very fine tidepooling area with abalone picking, skin diving, and rock fishing. It's also great exploring for older kids.

DRAKE'S BEACH. If you stay on Sir Francis Drake out of Inverness, turning left, the road will take you to two beaches on the ocean side, the lighthouse at the very point of Point Reyes, the Fish Docks at the opposite end of the point, and Drake's Beach.

For the first-time visitor, it's best to go directly to the Drake's Beach Visitor Center to get your bearings. Drake's Beach offers swimming, clamming in the estuary (a little down the beach), and surf fishing along the whole dramatic length of it. A lifeguard stands on duty during the summer, and, all considered, this beach offers so much that you may not wish to go farther.

The whole Point Reyes area is wonderful. The only thing to remember is that distances in this countryside are deceiving. Drake's Bay is only thirty miles north of San Francisco on the map, but it is a good two-hour drive to get there, because of two-laned, twisting roads.

Tomales Bay to Bodega Bay

From OLEMA through the little town of POINT REYES STATION you continue on Highway 1 up the east side of TOMALES BAY. Tomales Bay provides good fishing grounds and there are several commercial places, restaurants, bait shops, and boat rental and launching places between here and the city of TOMALES. There is good clamming all along this area, and if you stop in the town of MARSHALL or BLAKE'S LODGE, or NICK'S COVE (or any of the other places for that matter) you'll get reliable information about what to fish for, how, and where.

DILLON BEACH. At Tomales, turn left on the Dillon Beach Road to Dillon Beach. There are several resorts here. LAWSON'S LANDING has barges that take you out in the bay for clamming at low tides. There are party boats working this segment of shore, too. A small fee is charged for parking on the private beach at Lawson's Landing, but it's wide and clean and the parking attendants can tell you where the best local fishing and clamming spots are.

Highway 1 veers inland from Tomales, then returns to the coastline at Bodega Bay.

BODEGA BAY is the picturesque commercial fishing port and sport fishing center that became incidentally known for its winged wildlife when Alfred Hitchcock filmed *The Birds* here. In town, there are party-boat fishing and fishing from a private pier. Clamming, surf fishing, skin diving, surf netting, as well as tide-pooling, beachcombing, and all the rest of the beach sports are available. There is camping on DOREN BEACH COUNTY PARK, a sand spit at the entrance to BODEGA HARBOR. This area is extremely rich in marine animals and birds. The University of California maintains the Bodega Marine Laboratory on the ocean side of Bodega Head.

Bodega Bay to Russian River.

There are ten miles of state beaches from Bodega Bay to the mouth of the RUSSIAN RIVER. The headquarters are located at SALMON BEACH, with full camping facilities at WRIGHTS' BEACH. This is one of the most scenic stretches of coastline found anywhere in the world. The surf is dangerous though, so don't even think of swimming in it. It is great beachcombing country, not only for driftwood and jade, but also for ambergris (the protective plug that forms in a whale's gut around sharp squid beaks and other foreign objects and is used as a fixative in making the most expensive perfumes).

RUSSIAN RIVER. For generations, it's always been known to San Franciscans as "The River." It's a sort of backward resort, when you think of it. Whereas in most big cities, the heat of summer is so unbearable that the considerate father ships mother and kids to the mountains or seashore to escape it, San Francisco is so cold and foggy during the summer that everyone escaped to "The River" to get some sunshine and swim out of doors. This was even before the bridges made the trip easy. The tradition persists, and Russian River is still a major Northern California resort area.

You can reach Russian River either by Highway 1 (which is the way this book approached it), or by taking Highway 101 past Santa Rosa to either the Guerneville Road or the River Road turnoff. This route covers about seventy miles on good highways— an hour-and-a-half trip.

The main attraction for kids on Russian River is the river itself. Along the twenty-five miles of resort area, there are an uncounted number of swimming beaches and swimming holes. Some are private, some public. The river is a smallish one, which is a blessing in that it allows canoeing but prevents the excessive use of motorboats. The string of resorts along the river has been here for a long time, so there are many amusements (miniature golf and others) for kids. Most families who come here have cabins or rent them, but with the good roads, anyone can come up for a day's outing on the river, and it will not be a major trip. Some things to see in the area are as follows:

ARMSTRONG REDWOODS STATE RESERVE. A few miles above Guerneville, this southernmost corner of the AUSTIN CREEK STATE RECREATION AREA offers campsites, waterfalls along a charming creek, and good rock hounding.

FORT ROSS HISTORICAL PARK. About nine miles above Jenner, Fort Ross was the southernmost Russian colony on the West Coast. In the early nineteenth century (from about 1802 to 1841, when they sold the property to Captain Sutter of gold-discovery fame) imperial Russia flew her flag over this part of California. It was a fur-trading outpost, remaining until the sea otter was wiped out. The original fort burned, the replica burned again a few years ago, and yet another replica is being built.

OCCIDENTAL. This has to be one of the most curious towns in America—in a way that appeals to hungry kids. Occidental is a wide spot in the road between Sebastopol and Monte Rio along the Bohemian Highway. The town is built around three historic restaurants which, for the whole of their existence, from the days when they catered to turn-of-the-century loggers until now, have tried to find one person who could eat everything they put in front of him in one of their famous family dinners. They are still trying. The meals are Italian, wonderfully good, and reasonable. On Thanksgiving and Christmas, the restaurants are reserved months in advance by San Francisco families who are willing to drive seventy miles each way to eat there. Now, that's food!

SANTA ROSA is a bustling town with one famous son. Although I've avoided many "uplifting" tourist attractions, because nine times out of ten they bore kids to death, one should at least drift by the LUTHER BURBANK MEMORIAL GARDEN (on Santa Rosa Avenue between Sonoma Avenue and Charles Street).

Burbank was the typical "American inventor." As Cyrus McCormick worked with farm machinery and Thomas Edison with electricity, Burbank worked with plants. These men were not scientists looking for general principles; they were looking for what worked. All were acclaimed for their discoveries and inventions but were put down by the scientific community of their day as "tinkerers." Burbank's first "invention" was a revolutionary new potato. Subsequently he laid the groundwork (!) for developing many of the fruits and vegetables the world eats today. He did this mainly on his own. None of these guys had a Ph.D., and probably right at this minute "American inventors" of their same independent ilk are working to develop no-pollution engines, better wind- and solar-powered generating sources, more farm production, better houses, cheaper appliances. There is always a place for them in our society.

Russian River to Calistoga

The River Road from Russian River across Highway 101 to Calistoga takes you into a different world. It's dominated by the range of hills above San Pablo Bay, from Kenwood down to Sonoma, known as the VALLEY OF THE MOON, across the Mount Saint Helena and the Napa Valley. This is all volcanic area. Hot springs still sputter up with their curing water and mud, and the scenery is dramatic. The best route for kids is straight across the hills to Calistoga. This is great rock-hounding territory, and just outside Calistoga, on the road from Russian River is the Petrified Forest.

The PETRIFIED FOREST is commercial, with a modest entrance fee. The fine thing about it is that fossilized trees, so perfectly preserved that you can't tell six-million-year-old chunks of redwood from those freshly cut for firewood,* were buried by an eruption from the dormant volcano you can see around a turn in the road. These trees aren't agatized, making beautiful jewelry, but seemingly turned to stone by a wave of a magician's wand. There are excavations into the tufa, displaying trees over a hundred feet long, knocked down by the blast of the eruption and buried and fossilized.

CALISTOGA is one the flanks of Mount Saint Helena and is a health spa, full of elderly health-seekers. We arrived late in the afternoon and looked for a motel one day in late spring. The only place with a vacancy asked $20.00 a night for the three of us. I thought that was a bit steep for a little town but took it so we wouldn't have to look further. It turned out we had a living room–dinette area (a crazy breakfront turned into stove, sink, and refrigerator), a double bed in a small room separated by a room divider, and a couch that made into a bed for our four-year-old. Then we opened the bathroom door. That one room was as large as the other part of the accommodations—a huge, white-tiled place with a three-foot-deep sunken tub (two steps down) at least six by six. The bath-

---

*Figuratively speaking, of course. Food cooked over a red-wood fire is poisonous.

room was flooded by sun lamps. It took twenty minutes to fill the tub with hot mineral water and we immediately put on our swim suits, blew up the beach ball, and had one heck of a time splashing around.

Early mountain men and explorers in this area have reported seeing aged grizzly bears up to their necks in the healing muds of Calistoga. The grizzly is gone forever from California, but the town of Calistoga attests to his innate wisdom.

Calistoga to Sonoma

Calistoga lies in the NAPA VALLEY, on either side of which stretch ranges of hills. If you're there on a weekend, stop at the gas station just out of the middle of the town. The hills make for perfect sail-plane flying and you can examine the gliders closely, then watch them being towed up into the updrafts and sail free.

There are two ways down to SONOMA. One way is to retrace past the Petrified Forest and follow Route 12 through the Valley of the Moon. If any of you are interested in Jack London, you can visit his Wolf House outside Glen Ellen. Kids tend to like the Napa Valley route better, though. It follows the wine country through a beautiful broad valley. The huge propellers you see in the fields are fired up when frost threatens the grape crop. In the south they use smudge pots to keep the temperature above freezing when the fruit is about to be harvested. Here they use wind machines to draw the warmer air down.

Not only is this valley beautiful, but in the middle of it flows the Napa River. You can reach it from almost any road heading left off the highway. The river is really great rock-hounding ground. For eons it has washed rocks down from Mount St. Helena, and you can pick up big chunks of obsidian (glassy, black, beautiful stuff), common opal, and mineral specimens you'd pay a few bucks for in a lapidary store. This is one of the places the stores collect their merchandise.

You'll see a great many stone fences. The stones were cleared from the fields by imported Chinese labor a hundred years ago. The stately mansions you see along the side of the road are usually the headquarters of wineries. In the Santa Clara Valley around San Jose, the area around Russian River, and here, there are many famous wineries that have open house and guided tours. They're all advertised very well by signs along the road so you won't miss them if you want to visit.

OLD BALE MILL. Just north of St. Helena, you'll be intrigued by one of the hugest wooden water wheels you've ever seen. This is the Old Bale Mill, and it is open to the public, with picnic grounds around it. There's no charge for the tours through the mill.

SONOMA. Figuring prominently in pre–Gold Rush California history, many of the historic buildings of early-nineteenth-century Sonoma have been preserved in the SONOMA STATE HISTORIC PARK. Scattered around the plaza in the middle of town are adobe churches, residences, and businesses. A half-mile away is the home of General Vallejo, who was a leader in Mexican California and helped to guide California to American statehood. Sonoma is a lovely little town and a good place to walk around. It's one of the few authentic historic tourist features that hasn't gone commercial.

SONOMA GASLIGHT AND WESTERN RAILROAD. Weekends and holidays, 10:30 AM-5:30 PM; every day but Monday from June 17 to Labor Day, 1 PM–5:30 PM Modest charge for the train ride.

One of the very few commercial kids' attractions between San Francisco and Russian River, this miniature railroad delights the little ones. Miniature railroad cars pulled by a steam engine wind through ten acres of tracks, across beautifully maintained grounds.

To return to San Francisco, take Route 12 to 121 and follow the signs—it's about forty-five minutes to San Francisco.

22

East Bay

OAKLAND AND THE EAST BAY have taken a lot of abuse over the years from San Francisco. While San Francisco has always been a sophisticated, cosmopolitan metropolis, Oakland has always been a rather nothing town. It's not that Oakland is so bad itself, it's that it suffers from comparison. If it were located anywhere but just across the Bay from San Francisco, Oakland and its neighboring cities would have a much better reputation than they do. For all the gibes and jokes, though, Oakland and the East Bay have some wonderful places. The only difficulty in reaching them is understanding the freeway system. It is hoped that the directions given here will get you there without your getting lost.

Lake Merritt

There are three very special features on the north and south sides of LAKE MERRITT (one of the most beautiful municipal lakes to be found anywhere). The north side has the wildlife refuge, boating facilities, a science center, and Fairyland. The Oakland Museum is located on the south side. Unfortunately, they are approached most directly from two different freeways. We'll look at the north side first.

198

To reach CHILDREN'S FAIRYLAND and ROTARY NATURAL SCIENCE CENTER, take the MacArthur Freeway (Route 580) from the Oakland side of the Bay Bridge, then take the Grand Avenue off-ramp. Parking is easier around the Science Center. Fairyland is a ten-minute walk from there, but elephant trains shuttle between the two parts of the park regularly (25¢ round trip), so if you have toddlers, you don't have to worry about carrying them.

ROTARY NATURAL SCIENCE CENTER AND WILDFOWL RESERVE. Lake Merritt was the first game reserve to be set aside by any legislature on the North American continent (in the 1870s). Today it remains a permanent refuge for some wildfowl and a stopping point for many varieties of migrating ducks and geese. Around the area here are some displays of native animals and birds and in the Center itself are found ecology displays and exhibits of plants and rocks. Feed for the birds can be purchased from vending machines and food for the kids can be had at a large snack bar (reasonable and good). There's a small play area for little kids, but it's nothing compared with Fairyland. If you follow the lake side from the refreshment stand, you'll find the sailboat house where boats can be rented. The main feeding time for the birds and animals is 3:30 PM.

CHILDREN'S FAIRYLAND. Either take the 25¢ shuttle or follow the road around. It's directly opposite the duck area through the gardening area. The walk along the road is very nice. Trees and bushes are labeled to let you identify what you're seeing. There's a sandy play area on the beach nearby and an old-fashioned bandstand. Fairyland is open every day during the school summer vacation, 10 AM–5:30 PM. September–November, open Wednesday–Sunday; November–March, weekends only (it's open on all school holidays); March–June, Wednesday–Sunday.

Admission: ages 13 and up, 50¢; 2–12, 25¢; under 2 free. No adult admitted without a child.

This is the best of the parks strictly for children in the Bay Area. It combines a sort of children's zoo with some rides and a whole lot of great things to slide down, climb on, and go through (pirate's-ship rigging, mazes, dragon slides). There are free puppet shows at 11 AM, 2 PM, and 4 PM; clown shows at 11:20 AM, 1 PM, and 3 PM. Any time we've gone, there always seemed to be something going on—pie-eating contests, festivals, pagents. This is a big place with lots to do, so plan for the afternoon at least. There is a snack bar here, and there are vending machines to feed the little animals and seals. I know of no other place where little kids especially get such a kick and parents enjoy themselves as well. Very highly recommended.

OAKLAND MUSEUM. Other side of Lake Merritt. From the Bridge, take the Nimitz Freeway (Route 17) to the Jackson Street exit. Go three stoplights to Oak and turn north. The Museum has parking space for two hundred cars, at 25¢ per hour. Hours are Tuesday–Sunday, 10 AM–5 PM (open Friday till 10). Closed Monday. Free.

This is one of the most amazing buildings in America, architecturally and culturally. It's three museums in one with a park on top. There are three levels with I don't know how many staircases. It's not hard to get confused here, so keep track of each other. The first level is devoted to California ecology and is an excellent example of how natural history museums should be built. Here, in beautifully meticulous dioramas, the incredible complexity of animal and plant life of California is exhibited. From the coastline plants and creatures through hills, deserts, and mountains, you can get a fine appreciation of this state and what kinds of beasts and vegetation are disturbed when man intrudes.

The second level is devoted to California history. Now, that might seem dry, but I don't think I've seen a more exciting museum anywhere. Instead of the exhibits' being shut away in remote cases, you can walk through them, even touch restored fire engines, and old carriages. California's Indian past is extremely rich and its European past dates from Queen Elizabeth and Sir Francis Drake.

The third level is an art gallery, covering the earliest California art to the most modern—with more modern represented than early works.

OAKLAND ZOO (in KNOWLAND STATE PARK). Take the MacArthur Freeway from the Bridge to the Golf Links Road–Ninety-eighth Avenue turnoff. This is about seven miles past the bridge—you'll know you're getting close when you've passed Mills College. The zoo is open daily, 10 AM–5 PM. Free.

This is a small but growing zoo with many attractions other zoos could copy. There are some rides and concessions near the entrance. The thing that dominates is the most immense gibbon cage I've seen anywhere—it must be four stories high. A miniature train takes you around the perimeter of the zoo and a "Jungle Lift" lifts you over the zoo and up into the hills.

The BABY ZOO (adults 75¢ children 2–15, 50¢) is supposed to be rated as one of the finest zoos of its type in the nation, and it is very fine, with nearly two-hundred animals available for touching and feeding, but I still prefer the children's zoo in San Francisco—perhaps it's the rather steep admission charge that puts me off. Still, the whole zoo is nice and new.

In and Near Berkeley

These are not listed by importance but because they use the same off-ramp from the Freeway. (That's important because you can get completely lost over there if you don't know your way around.) For all three of these fine places, you take Highway 80 from the bridge and head north toward Sacramento. For all three, you take the University Avenue off-ramp.

BERKLEY MARINA. This is a stunning new development offering great sea-level views of San Francisco, a fine small-craft marina, good restaurants, and an extremely long public fishing pier into the Bay. Party boats operate out of here, and there are bait and fishing tackle shops. The Berkeley Marina is just abuilding, and in the future, there will be a golf course and several parks here, as well as a heliport and a hovercraft port. It's a grand drive now, just as it is, and the fishing pier, like all other public fishing piers, requires no fishing license.

LOWIE MUSEUM OF ANTHROPOLOGY. University of California at Berkeley. University Avenue runs smack into the University of California—Berkeley campus. The campus is bordered by Hearst on the north, Oxford on the west (University ends at Oxford) and Bancroft on the south. The Lowie Museum is just off Bancroft near Telegraph and College. Turn right on Oxford and left on Bancroft, Channing, or Durant and try to find a parking space. At both Telegraph and College, there are comprehensive maps of the University and you'll have no trouble finding it. (There's more apt to be a problem finding parking space.)

The Lowie Museum is a showcase of the extensive work done over the years by the world-famous Anthropology Department of the University of California. Anthropology means the study of man, and there are exhibits covering the whole of mankind all over the globe; technical displays of how anthropologists work and general displays showing the arts and crafts of many peoples. One of the most interesting displays is about Ishi, the last stone-age Indian in America. You look at the chipped arrowheads, the bows and arrows, the working equipment of a hunter-gatherer, and conclude that this is prehistoric stuff, made in the old days before white men came to North America. But that's not the case at all. These things were made by Ishi between 1911, when he was starved out of the hills near Mount Lassen, and 1916 when he died of tuberculosis in San Francisco. Ishi was the last survivor of a remote tribe that was systematically wiped out by gold seekers, then by ranchers. After his mother and sister were lost (presumably drowned) in a wild flight from white men, he gave himself up and was taken to the Anthropology Department of the University (which then was near the Medical Center in San Francisco). These things were made while he was there. That was just sixty years ago. In 1916, men were flying through the air; automobiles were chugging around; the telephone, electric light, moving pictures, elevators, sky scrapers, and motorized farm machinery were common in an America with no new frontiers to conquer. In Northern California, though, was a man whose most vivid recollections were of how men lived ten thousand years before—amazing!

LAWRENCE HALL of SCIENCE. Take the University Avenue exit to the campus, turn left on Oxford, right on Hearst to Galey, then left up the hill on Rim Way (before you get to the stadium), then left to Centennial Drive. Most of these streets stop at the others mentioned; if you keep going uphill, you can't miss it.

This is a special place, especially if you are just becoming interested in science, say about eight and up (although there are things to interest six-year-olds). It's open every day except university holidays (which are the major holidays of the year—and a few extra). If in doubt, call 642-5132. Adults $1, students and senior citizens 50¢, children 12 and under 25¢; no charge for children under 6 when accompanied by adult.

This science center is named for Ernest Lawrence, the famed nuclear scientist, developer of the cyclotron, and Nobel Prize winner. In the entrance to the science hall is something for all—the parchment proclamations, medals and paraphernalia of a Nobel Prize–winner, which few people ever have an opportunity to examine. The center emphasizes physical science, which tends to be abstract. A myriad community projects are always in progress to train young scientists; they tend to be obscure unless you're involved in them but they are something for Bay Area families to look into. There is a magnificent physical sciences game room that is a complete joy to kids, a kind of scientific penny arcade or pinball parlor. Each machine (and they're complex things) amuses and educates at the same time. Shoot a ball at an unseen target and guess which unseen shape has deflected the ball! Match the optical illusion! Can you bend the light wave? Make your own chromatic chemical analysis! There must be forty or fifty machines.

MOUNT DIABLO STATE PARK. Mount Diablo is the highest point, at 3,849 feet above sea level, in north-central California. It has the unique distinction of overlooking more territory in clear-weather viewing than any other place in the world, with the exception of Mount Kilimanjaro in Africa (which is 19,000 feet high). There have been panoramic overlapping photographs taken from this peak (admittedly in pre-smog days) that have included Mount Shasta in the north, the Sierra to the east, Mount Whitney to the south, and a view to the west nearly one hundred miles out to sea. Forty thousand square miles of area, land and sea! But in these days of industrial pollution and automobile-created smog, you're lucky if you get a clear look at five thousand or ten thousand square miles of Bay and Central Valley spread beneath you. The best time for super viewing is an early spring morning just after a big rainstorm from the north has swept through.

To reach Mount Diablo, take Route 580 to Route 24 as if you were going to Walnut Creek. Turn right on Highway 680 going south and take the turnoff around Danville—the route from 680 is very well marked. There is a small entrance fee and, if you have a dog, it must be on a leash and wearing a rabies tag. There are myriad viewpoints and picnic areas on the way up to the summit (Get a map of the park where you pay your fee.) At the top there is a snack bar where hot coffee, hot chocolate, and hot soup are served (along with sandwiches). The hot drinks are welcome because the air is apt to be nippy. You pass through several zones of vegetation on your way up, and there is good rock hounding from the slopes up (since the area is a state park, nothing may be removed), including both vertebrate (saber tooth tiger, for example) and invertebrate fossils—examine the stones with which the summit house is constructed. There's a lot of exploring to be done on Mount Diablo and it's good for the whole family.

East Bay Regional Parks

The East Bay Regional Park System (a multi-county effort) puts some twenty-six thousand acres of wilderness area, developed park facilities, swimming, boating, nature study, hiking, equestrian trails, picnicking, and lesser features within a short drive of every Bay area resident. Stretching roughly in a line from Berkeley–Lafayette in the north to Newark–Livermore in the south, each park offers its own particular attractions and the whole provides a new place for family outings for a week of Sundays. We'll start at the north and work our way south.

TILDEN PARK. Berkeley. From University Avenue, turn left on Spruce to Grizzly Peak Boulevard entrance.

This is an excellent exploring park—you find something different every time you visit. (On our last visit, a cricket match was in progress near the merry-go-round—the first such I've seen in America.) In separate parts, there are merry-go-rounds and pony rides; swimming, fishing, picnicking, and nature trails. Three very good things are the Little Farm, the steam railroad, and the California Botanical Garden.

The LITTLE FARM not only has the usual pettable farm animals, but also a collection of antique farm equipment—cradle scythes, hay rakes, harrows—and a windmill (no longer pumping water) low enough to the ground to show how windmills worked. A new ecology center is being built near the Little Farm.

Near the merry-go-round is a lake with swimming, fishing and picnicking. (Parking is available near the lake for a slight fee—or walk down from the merry-go-around.)

The steam railroad is the pet project of East Bay railroad buffs. It offers a good ride on miniature cars pulled by a genuine coal-burning miniature locomotive. A new, smaller gauge railroad center is being constructed farther down the hill (you'll see it on your trip) and out-of-town railroad enthusiasts can find local people working there on weekends.

The CALIFORNIA NATIVE PLANT BOTANICAL GARDEN lets you walk through all the flora of California. The garden includes most of the major plants, from weeds to grasses to bushes to trees that range from sea level through the hills, deserts, and mountains of California. Nearly every plant in the garden is labeled (with some exasperating exceptions) and you can finally identify all those plants you've seen and walked through but never been able to put a name to. The garden is divided into biotic zones so all plants of one region are close together.

BRIONES REGIONAL PARK. From Route 24 (as if you were going to Walnut Creek), take the Happy Valley Road to the Bear Creek Road to the entrance to the park.

Briones is wild country with excellent picnicking, nature study, and hiking. A friend who writes for *Field and Stream* and *Sports Afield* says this is the finest piece of wild land in the whole East Bay—he says that he has even seen bobcat there. Picnicking only, no camping.

LAKE TEMESCAL. Oakland. Take Route 24 (Walnut Creek) to Broadway exit. Turn left to Broadway Terrace and follow the signs.

A lovely lake in the Oakland Hills, Lake Temescal offers swimming, boating, and super picnic grounds. There is a children's playground there, but the main feature is the lake. It is cram full of bluegills. You can catch more fish faster here than anywhere I know of.

REDWOOD REGIONAL PARK. Take Route 24 to Warren Boulevard (Route 13 going south). Take the Skyline Boulevard exit from there.

This is a park of more than two thousand acres, with excellent hiking trails through second-growth redwoods. The original trees were logged off in the 1840s–1850s, some of the lumber going to Sutter's Fort, some to Mission San Jose, and some to Benicia, an early state capital.

Robert's Regional Recreational Area, within the larger park, has a heated outdoor swimming pool, wading pool, children's playground, and picnic grounds.

ANTHONY CHABOT REGIONAL PARK. Take MacArthur Freeway (Highway 580). For the north end (hiking, nature walks) take the Golf Links off-ramp through Oakland Zoo–Knowland Park. For the south end (marina on Lake Chabot) take the Estudillo Boulevard turnoff.

Anthony Chabot is a large, long park (nearly five thousand acres). The north end offers excellent hiking and picnicking. Lake Chabot lies in the south and offers boating and excellent lake fishing. There's an archery range and a marksmanship range (pistol, rifle, and trap shooting). There are also camping facilities. A tour boat circles the lake and with the "Stop and Go Tour," you can be let off at any of the four stops and be picked up in a later go-round. Check the limits and license requirements if you plan to fish.

Coyote Hills Park. Fremont. Take the Nimitz Freeway (Highway 17) to Fremont. (You'll pass San Leandro.) Take the Jarvis Avenue off-ramp to Newark Boulevard. Turn right to the Patterson Ranch Road and follow the signs.

Coyote Hills is a Bay-facing park with many things to see. There is an extensive marshland bird reserve (with huge numbers of all kind of birds—bring your binoculars); the hills facing the Bay have excellent updrafts, perfect for kite flying and model radio-operated glider operation; then there are the Bio-Sonar Laboratories and the Indian Shell Mounds.

This was a very popular spot for early Californian Indians and it has been estimated that the site was continuously occupied from 2,000 B.C. to the late 1800s. The mounds, kitchen middens, are just within the entrance to the park and are reserved to professional archaeologists. In 1973, tours were conducted by park naturalists to the mounds on the first Saturday of each month from March to October. You can check with the East Bay Regional Park District office in Oakland, phone 531-9300, for the 1974 schedule.

The Bio-Sonar Laboratory was a very important center where basic research was done on the ability of large sea mammals to "see" underwater with sound echos—sonar. The first Saturday of each month a naturalist or one of the Laboratory personnel conducts a tour, starting with the sea lions and seals, pointing out the differences and explaining some of their feeding, breeding, and life habits. You then go to the laboratory, which houses a huge tank with observation ports at eye level. The tank is acoustically "dead," made so by a complex array of sound baffles. There the scientists study just how fine the tuning of the sea beasts' sonar really is (and try to discover how they can tell the difference between a fine-scaled fish from a rough-scaled fish). In 1973, the tours were at noon, 1:30 PM, and 3 PM on the first Saturday of the month. Call the above number to make sure of the times.

DEL VALLE RECREATIONAL. AREA. Livermore. Take Highway 580 to Livermore. Take the Portola off-ramp and bear right to L Street, then left to South Livermore Drive; left again to Tesla, then to Mines Road. This takes you to Del Valle Road and the entrance to the park.

The main feature of this thirty-five-hundred-acre park is the five-mile-long Del Valle Lake. There are fishing, swimming, boating (boats available for rent), hiking, horseback riding, and family camping. There is a small day use charge ($1.50 per car at this writing) and a $2.50-per-car-overnight camping fee. A tour boat regularly plies the lake to take you to the various prime picnic and hiking areas. You can buy food, bait tackle, and firewood and rent boats at the park concession stand.

23

Shops for Kids

ONE OF THE best things a big city has to offer is its good and varied shops. Here you can browse through items that you usually have to send away for back home. It's tough on a young hobbyist to have the urge to make something and not have the material at hand. Waiting for things in the mail is a heartbreakingly tedious undertaking for kids, and when the stuff comes, often it doesn't *quite* measure up to expectations; at any rate, the first enthusiasm is gone. Before you start out, even when you're planning the trip, you might set aside a specific amount—and it should be something substantial, like fifteen or twenty dollars—earmarked solely for a favorite hobby. That way, when you see something you really want, it won't be an unexpected outlay from the family traveling money.

The following is a list of stores that cater to all the hobbies I can think of. These stores are in San Francisco or very near (Oakland, Berkeley, or San Jose). There are others I'm sure I've missed, and for that I apologize both to the good stores and the seekers after good stuff. Listed here also are toy, book, and specialty stores that, in the main, are found only in major cities and are adult- as well as child-oriented. (The Government Printing Office Book Store and Rand McNally are examples of unique stores.)

Following the shops is a listing of ethnic specialty

shops and restaurants, where the crafts, books, records, and food of "foreign" countries can be had. Kids, of course, are interested in their own personal family history and if their surname is German, Germany is likely to be their favorite foreign country. They might want to eat in a "real" German restaurant. Of course, all families might want to go to a genuine Philippine supermarket where they can buy banana ice cream imported from Manila.

All the sports from archery to pole vaulting are listed in the Sporting Goods section; all crafts from basket weaving to stained-glass-making are listed under Handicrafts. You'll probably notice that some hobbies and interests are missing. I don't know anything about really good automotive stuff or motorcycles— where to shop for customizing equipment—because I can just barely replace a cigarette lighter in my own car. For the gaps, consult the yellow pages.

Acting and Theater Arts

In small towns, you usually have to send away for your makeup, nose putty, false beards, and costume supplies. There are two stores here that handle all of it.

DANCE ART, 222 Powell Street, San Francisco.

ENCORE THEATRICAL SUPPLY CO., 5929 MacArthur Boulevard, Oakland.

Animals and Pets

San Francisco and the Bay area have some good stores where unusual pets may be found, as well as puppies and kitties.

THE HOUSE OF PETS, 135 Maiden Lane (oldest in the area), San Francisco.

AVES EXOTICA, 21688 Schillingsburg Avenue, San Jose. (Rare birds, wild animals.)

EAST BAY VIVARIUM, 1511 MacArthur Boulevard, Oakland. (Snakes, lizards, frogs, etcetera)

THE HERPETARIUM, 4200 Balboa Street, San Francisco. (Same thing.)

LAWTON PET SHOP, 2123 Irving Street, San Francisco. (Rare birds.)

AQUATIC PET SHOP, 1901 Fillmore Street, San Francisco.

Art

Every town has artist's materials for sale, but perhaps not as complete as these.

FLAX, 250 Sutter Street, San Francisco. (Perhaps the greatest variety of any.)

DIRTY RAINBOW ARTISTS' MATERIALS, 2514 Durant Avenue, Berkeley.

SAN FRANCISCO ART INSTITUTE Student Store, 800 Chestnut Street, San Francisco.

ARCHITECTURAL MODEL SUPPLIES CO., 361 Brannan Street, San Francisco. (Supplies and tools for making architectural models.)

MACPHERSON BROS., 730 Polk Street, San Francisco.

HOSHINO, 1541 Clement Street, San Francisco. (Fine Japanese papers, and batik and woodblock supplies.)

PARKVIEW G.E.T. DISCOUNT DEPARTMENT STORE, 11 Lakeshore Place, San Francisco (On Sloat Boulevard near the Zoo.)

STANDARD BRANDS, Serramonte Shopping Center, Daly City. (Off Highway 280.)

UNITED SURPLUS SALES, Jackson and Eleventh Streets, Oakland.

Astronomy

OPTICA B/C, 4100 MacArthur Boulevard, Oakland.
(Telescopes, mirror blanks and lenses, eye pieces,
sky maps.)

GOLDEN GATE PARK ACADEMY of SCIENCES,
San Francisco. (Some Pyrex mirror kits at the gift
stand at the Planetarium.)

Autographs

ROBERT KUHN, 720 Geary Street, San Francisco.
(Has the kind of autographs—and in the price
range—most kids collect—as well as coins and
fantastic memorabilia—World War I German helmets, for example.)

BURGER & EVANS, 3421 Geary Boulevard, San
Francisco. (More expensive—wider range.)

Boats and Ships

Even if you don't own a boat, these two old-time
ships' chandlers are loads of fun to walk through—
everything from radar to lifeboat rations—fittings for
crafts of all sizes.

JOHNSON & JOSEPH Co., 496 Jefferson Street, Fisherman's Wharf, San Francisco

WEEKS-HOWE-EMERSON, 645 Howard Street, San
Francisco.

Books

At last count, there were over two-hundred bookstores in San Francisco. The range of subject matter is

simply incredible. Obviously, I am slighting the subject, by including only two bookstores as special for kids. Consult the yellow pages if you have a special interest.

THE GOVERNMENT PRINTING OFFICE BOOK STORE, Federal Office Building, 450 Golden Gate Avenue, San Francisco. This is a super-special bookstore. It's one of the rare retail outlets of Government Printing Office publications—which, as you know puts out pamphlets and books on every subject under the sun. There are books that teach you how to fly a helicopter and how to start your own catfish farm; military survival books—in case you are shot down in the forest-jungle-desert; books on how to slaughter your own hog, on the history of various Indian tribes, and on building your own house. The books are well made and extremely cheap. Some of the best buys are the beautiful books of photographs taken on the various space missions. The whole family should take advantage of one of the very finest of all the government services.

STACEY'S BOOKSTORE, 581 Market Street, San Francisco. This is a general and paperback store that specializes in scientific books. You're apt to find a better selection of these special books than in any book store back home.

Chemistry

The only place I've been able to find replacements for kids' chemistry sets is:

THE EMPORIUM, 835 Market Street, Hobby Department, San Francisco and branches.

Coins

I'm not at all an expert, but you can try these shops.

THE EMPORIUM, 835 Market Street, Coin and Stamp Department, San Francisco.

ROBERT R. JOHNSON, INC., 353 Geary Street, San Francisco.

CASH COINS, 22 Peace Plaza, Japantown, San Francisco.

CAMINO COIN CO., 5 Thirty-seventh Avenue (at El Camino Real), San Mateo.

WITTER COINS, 382 Bush Street, San Francisco

COIN GALLERY OF SAN FRANCISCO, 62 Post Street, San Francisco.

Dolls

THUMBELINA, 2338 Clement Street, San Francisco.

MARK FARMER CO., INC., 36 Washington Avenue, Richmond.

NICOLE DOLLS, 251 Grant Avenue, San Francisco.

ANTIQUES LTD., 3294 Sacramento Street, San Francisco.

Electronics

The best place for kids interested in electronics is the 1200 block of Market Street in San Francisco. Four stores in a row deal both in new parts and equipment and in used equipment and surplus electronics pieces.

Fish

A friend who raises tropical fish recommends the following:

TROPICAL FISH HUT, 3809 Geary Boulevard, San Francisco.

B & H TROPICAL FISH, 3277 Mission Street, San Francisco.

AQUATIC SPECIALTIES, 1255 Vicente Street, San Francisco.

DELLBROOK TROPICALS, 401A Judah Street, San Francisco.

NIPPON GOLDFISH CO., 3109 Geary Boulevard, San Francisco.

BLUE LAGOON, 1644A Irving Street, San Francisco.

Handicrafts

This is a huge subject which blends with art; indeed all the shops mentioned in the Art section handle some craft supplies as well, especially tools. The shops listed in this section are specialists in their own field and have selections of materials not usually available outside big towns. I've tried to include sources of supply for the handicrafts most kids (and their parents) might be involved with. I'm sure I've missed some, and some supply houses I simply haven't been able to find (for example, glassblowing supplies). Most kids, when they're old enough to get into a craft hobby—or any other hobby—are serious about it and want serious stuff to work with. Kits are great to begin with—to learn the basic steps—but kids enjoy the "real thing"—the raw materials to go it on their own. These shops will supply them.

General

AMERICAN HANDICRAFTS, 2920 Geary Boulevard, San Francisco. This store is a retail outlet of one of the biggest handicraft suppliers in the country. The store stocks raw material for work in decoupage, candle-making (especially molds), beadwork, jewelry, plastics, copper blanks for metalwork, string and cord for macramé, indeed all small crafts. It has channel lead for stained-glass work and many, many kits for beginners in all kinds of crafts. It is super-general, handling most of the things that kids taking the first step into any given craft can use. It's also geared to the one-time craftsman, which means that though it's broad, it's not very deep.

> MacPherson Bros., 730 Polk Street, San Francisco. A good line of arts-and-crafts supplies without so much emphasis on kits.
>
> Fantasy Import Mart, 1029 Market Street, San Francisco.

Basketry

Supplies for this craft are sometimes hard to find. Here are two shops in San Francisco.

> Three Bags Full, 1035 Guerrero Street.
>
> Lun On Co., 771 Sacramento Street (off Grant Avenue, Chinatown). (Basketry material, rattan, chair caning supplies, and bamboos.)

Bookbinding

> Artisan Bookbinding Supplies, 1215 Ninth Avenue, Oakland.

Candles

> Yaley Enterprises, 129 Sylvester Street, South San Francisco.
>
> The Candle Shop, 401 Balboa Street, San Francisco.
>
> Importex, 1355 Market Street, San Francisco.
>
> Mosaic International, 1806 Polk Street, San Francisco. (See also page 219.)

Jewelry

Most of the general-handicraft shops and nearly all the lapidary shops have findings, blands, gold and silver wire, copper enamel equipment, etc. Check them also.

> Craft Jewelry Supplies, 938 Mission Street, San Francisco.
>
> Yone Beads, 478 Union Street, San Francisco.

(These two shops also have an immense assortment of beads for jewelry and macramé.)

SEABROOK JEWELERY & LAPIDARY SUPPLY, 2829 Bridgeway, Sausalito.

OUR THING, 4207 Geary Boulevard, San Francisco.

PACIFIC HOME & FOREIGN TRADE, 1338 Mission Street, San Francisco.

Knitting, Sewing, Needlecraft, Rug-making, Weaving, Macramé

Fabrics

CHANDLER'S WARP 'N WOOF FABRICS, 90 Stonestown Mall, San Francisco.

BRITEX FABRICS, 146 Geary Street, San Francisco.

BLACK SHEEP, Cannery, 2801 Leavenworth Street, San Francisco.

HOME YARDAGE, 3245 Geary Boulevard, San Francisco.

Yards, Dyes, Equipment

THREE BAGS FULL, 1035 Guerrero Street, San Francisco.

CONTEMPORARY YARN CRAFTS, 3819 Seventeenth Street, San Francisco.

DHARMA TRADING CO., 1952 University Avenue, Berkeley.

THE KNITTERY, 2040 Union Street, San Francisco.

YARN GARDEN, 3061 Sacramento Street, San Francisco.

THE VILLAGE SHEEP, 2005 Bridgeway, Sausalito.

MERIBEE NEEDLECRAFT CO., 2901 Geary Boulevard, San Francisco.

BLACK GLEN HANDWOVEN TEXTILES LOCAL COLOR, 1414 Grant Avenue, San Francisco.

Leather

TANDY LEATHERCRAFT, 1310 Mission Street, San Francisco.

MACPHERSON BROS., 730 Polk Street, San Francisco.

Body-kiting at Ocean Beach is just one of the unexpected things that can appear out of the blue in San Francisco. (See Chapter 4.)

All photos by James Barber.

"The Exploratorium is a collection of mechanical, physical, and technical devices that trick you, test you, and help you discover this complicated world." (See Chapter 10.)

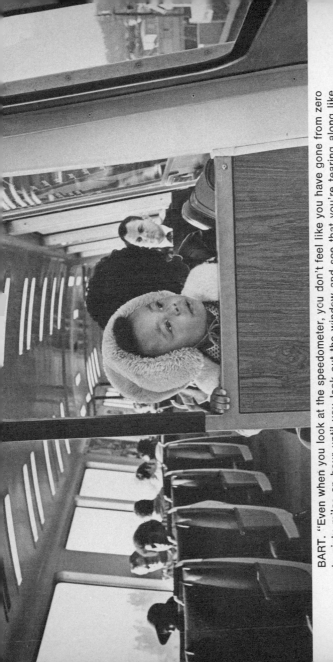

BART. "Even when you look at the speedometer, you don't feel like you have gone from zero to sixty miles an hour until you look out the window and see that you're tearing along like crazy." (See Chapter 17.)

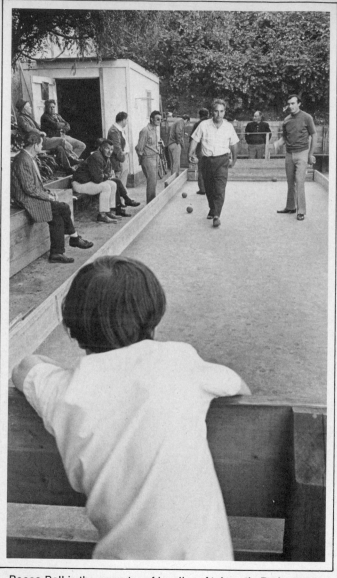

Bocce Ball is the ancestor of bowling. At Aquatic Park you can watch this exciting game which is rarely seen in America. (See Chapter 1.)

You can pet the animals at Children's Zoo, or ride a Merry-Go-Round, or climb an old railroad engine, depending on the mood you're in. (See Chapter 9.)

In Ghiradelli Square there's a shop entirely devoted to kites. There are cheap kites and forty-foot-long dragon kites that sell for over $100. You can buy a kite there, and fly it on the beach across the street. (See Chapter 23.)

Every time you visit the *Wapama* you see that something new has been added which gives you a new look at what it was like to travel by coastal steamer at the turn of the century. (See Chapter 1.)

The Vaillancourt Fountain. "It's absurd, but it's one of the few fountains in the world that invites you to walk in, on, and through it, getting nearly splashed at every turn and hissed at with steam with its own feeling of danger and mystery." (See Chapter 6.)

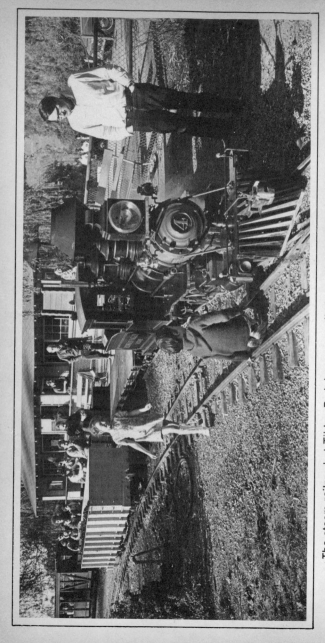

The steam railroad at Tilden Park has cars pulled by a genuine coal-burning miniature loco-motive. Even before you board, you know it's a great ride. (See Chapter 22.)

LEATHER, ETC., & THINGS, 752 Columbus Avenue, San Francisco.

Mosaics
MOSAIC INTERNATIONAL, 1806 Polk Street, San Francisco.

Stained Glass
LUCAS, 152 Helena Street, San Francisco (Stained-glass works; sells scrap stained glass by weight.)

THE STAINED GLASS SHOP, 2025 Seventeenth Street, San Francisco.

Woodworking
It's often a hard for woodworkers, carvers, etc. to find exotic hardwoods. Here are three outlets.

CALIFORNIA COMPANY HARDWOODS, INC., 1648 Airport Boulevard, Santa Rosa, (California hardwoods, redwood and redwood and madrone burls, walnut, etcetera.)

MCBEATH HARDWOOD Co., 2510 Oakdale, San Francisco. (General hardwood dealer.)

SOUTHERN LUMBER Co., 1402 South First Street, San Jose. (Exotic woods—ebony, rosewood, mahoganies, etcetera.)

And That Ends Handicrafts.

Kites

Kites are a special kind of device. They are partly toy and partly very serious wind engines: you can go in many directions with kites. Kids play with the little ones and the likes of Alexander Graham Bell experimented with huge ones.

COME FLY A KITE in Ghirardelli Square is the only shop I know of entirely devoted to kites. Here are flat, bowed, box, tetrahedron, parawing, and parafoil kites from all over. You'll see little butterfly kites from Japan and plastic soaring bird kites from

Germany; simple kites suitable for three-year-olds and complex ones that warn you that in the hands of three-year-olds these kites will be snatched to the heavens. There are cheap kites and forty-foot-long dragon kites that sell for over one hundred dollars. You'll find kite string (of various tensile strengths), kite paper, kite sticks, kite reels, and kite books. If you don't find the kind of kite you want, they can tell you where to find the person who will make it for you. In 1973, a new world's record was made by a group that put a kite up ten miles in the air. (The previous record was six miles.)

Lapidary

With such a wealth of minerals to be found in California and the surrounding states, it's not surprising that there is tremendous interest in the hobby of working with rocks. There are many fine shops that sell not only rock-cutting and -polishing equipment but also mineral specimens themselves to be displayed as works of art in the home. One such store is ARTHUR COURT DESIGNS, 888 North Point Street, San Francisco (across from Ghirardelli Square). I mention this store especially because of a unique item I've seen nowhere else. It's a six "volume" set of fossils packaged like a set of books. The set covers fish (with a little fossil fish), ferns, dinosaurs (a section of a dinosaur bone), sharks, trilobites, and ammonites. Each has a nicely mounted fossil and a booklet covering the geology of its own particular era. The whole set sells for $42.50, but each "book" can be bought separately. A booklet with a specimen mounted simply on a card sells for $4.95 for the fish and $2.95 for the others. For an Easter gift, I bought my boy, who is very deep into dinosaurs, one of the dinosaur cards and he almost fell on his head to imagine he owned a piece of a real dinosaur!

The shops listed are places for both the casual rock hound and the serious hobbyist. To my mind, this is one of the finest of hobbies. It takes a little research to know where to go find good rocks; exercise and good luck to find a nice specimen and then patience and careful manual work to finish it into what becomes for each a work of art. To cap it off, each polished bit of rock has built into it all the memories and experiences of what went before. No wonder it's such a satisfying hobby.

LAPIDARY CENTER, 4114 Judah Street, San Francisco. (Biggest store in town—also conducts classes.)

MINING AND LAPIDARY INDUSTRIES, 63 Eleventh Street, San Francisco. (Second largest—much prospecting equipment.)

FRANCIS J. SPERISEN, 166 Geary Street, Room 152 San Francisco. (For adult workers in jewelry—precious stones.)

GEMS & JEWELS, 2297A Market Street, San Francisco.

GOLDEN CITY JEWELRY & LAPIDARY, 5240 Mission Street, San Francisco.

BELMONT LAPIDARY SUPPLY, 740 El Camino Real, Belmont.

BINKLEY'S LAPIDARY SUPPLY, 2202 Lincoln Avenue, San Jose.

GOLDEN STATE GEMS, 22475 Maple Court, Hayward.

FRAZIER'S MINERALS & LAPIDARY, 1724 University Avenue, Berkeley.

TAM JEWELRY SUPPLIERS, 30 Miller Avenue, Mill Valley.

Magic

THE HOUSE OF MAGIC at 2025 Chestnut Street, San Francisco, is the unofficial headquarters of Bay area magicians. They sell everything from hand tricks, scarfs, cards, rings and novelty items to stage production effects, and can have any production number you dream up built for you. If you are really interested in Magic, you might consider going to TURK MURPHY'S EARTHQUAKE McGOON'S at 630 Clay Street (half a block down from the Portsmouth Square garage at Kearny Street). Turk Murphy's is a nightclub, and kids old enough not to disturb the other patrons will enjoy it. Upstairs, Turk Murphy holds forth with his world-famous Dixieland jazz band. Downstairs is his Magic Cellar. Through some quirk, he acquired the properties of Carter the Great, a famous stage magician. In vaudeville days Carter the Great toured the world with a company of sixteen people and thirty tons of equipment and costumes. Some of the more spectacular stage productions and a lot of smaller magic stuff is displayed here in a veritable magic museum. While Turk plays upstairs, a rotating group of foreign and local magicians performs downstairs right next to the "Disappearing Elephant Effect."

At this writing, there is an entrance charge of $1 and a minimum of $3.50 per person, but where else can you get great music and great magic all in one, at any price?

Maps

Two unusual stores for budding geographers are:

DEPARTMENT OF INTERIOR GEOLOGICAL SURVEY DEPARTMENT, 555 Battery Street, San Francisco.

Another good government outlet, the map bookstore, sells definitive geological plans of the six Western states. Weekdays, 8 AM–4:30 PM.

RAND McNALLY & Co., 206 Sansome Street, San Francisco. (One of *their* few retail outlets. Maps, books of maps, raised plastic physical maps, globes.)

Models

This section deals with directioning model-builders, plane, train, boat, and car enthusiasts to suppliers, but I must first mention the layout of the EAST BAY MODEL ENGINEERS SOCIETY at 4075 Halleck Street in Oakland. To get there, cross the Bay Bridge and take Highway 580 to the West Street turnoff, then go straight to San Pablo Avenue and take a right. Turn right again onto Park avenue and go past City Hall, then left onto Halleck. You can't miss it, the entrance is the back of a caboose.

Their big Open House is in the fall of the year around October, but it's open to the public the third Friday of every month 7:30–10 P.M. (Their phone number is 658-3537 if you want additional information.)

No matter what your particular model persuasion, you must see this as the epitome of what all modelists hold dear: perfection in reduction in scale; perfection in craftsmanship; perfection in the environment in which the models operate.

This is the largest scale-model railroad layout on exhibit under one roof in the world. There are two sections, the main one 63 x 100 feet, the one in the rear, 33 x 80 feet—and it is magnificent. Freight trains, mountain trains, steamliners, interurban trolleys are all going around and through the most meticulously modeled scenery (the bridges are fantastic in detail), controlled by a central yard that seems as complex as the Chicago yards. The society has been in operation since 1934 and the membership comes from all walks of life.

The best place to see model boats, both sail and motor is at Spreckels' Lake in Golden Gate Park on a weekend morning. The SAN FRANCISCO MODEL YACHT CLUB center is just off the lake and you can stop there to pick up hints about boats. From what

I've been able to find out, most of the model airplane activity is down on the peninsula around the general San Jose area. The shops listed here can give you information about meets, clubs, and what's happening in that field.

BILL'S TERMINAL TRAINATORIUM, 2049 Market Street, San Francisco.

NORIEGA HOBBY SHOP, 3917 Noriega Street, San Francisco.

FRANCISCAN HOBBIES, 1935 Ocean Avenue, San Francisco.

PAT'S HOUSE OF HOBBIES, 5186 Mission Street, San Francisco.

The larger good toy stores—F. A. O. SCHWARTZ, EMPORIUM, KING NORMAN'S TOYS, JEFFREY'S TOYS at Ghirardelli Square also have excellent model-building kits and some have materials as well. The foregoing doesn't seem like much of a list, but, from my information, these are where serious hobbyists begin.

Music

Most musicians know where to buy their instruments, but have trouble getting sheet music that's any way out of the ordinary. Here's some suggestions.

SHERMAN & CLAY, 141 Kearny Street, San Francisco.

BUCKNER'S MUSIC SUPPLIES, 1828 Clement Street, San Francisco.

BYRON HOYT SHEET MUSIC SERVICE, 190 Tenth Street, San Francisco

Photography

This is a big subject and some big stores in the area are:

BROOKS CAMERAS, 45 Kearny Street, San Francisco.

ADOLPH GASSER, 5733 Geary Boulevard, San Francisco.

SAN FRANCISCO CAMERA, 923 Market Street, San Francisco.

SCHAEFER'S CAMERAS, 110 Kearny Street, San Francisco.

Sporting Goods

Home-town shops carry most stuff: golf, tennis, footballs, basketballs, baseballs, and that kind of equipment. We have special shops here, though, that might not be so easy to come by—at least browse through—in a small town.

General

ABERCROMBIE & FITCH 220 Post Street, San Francisco. Now, this is a special shop. It's the *bon ton* of sporting goods that offers the little things that make a trip into the fields and streams a delight—such as imported wickerware picnic baskets—I mean, why carry your chicken sandwich in your pocket when you can have your butler carry the whole bird in the basket, with china and silver as well? Why boom away at a rabbit with a Sears Roebuck serviceable shotgun when you can buy an elegant one here, engraved and silver mounted? The point is that there aren't many shops like this. All their things aren't super-expensive, but all their things are first-rate. It's a great place to browse through.

DAVE SULLIVAN'S SPORT SHOP, 5323 Geary Boulevard. Here is everything from freeze-dried backpacking foods to guns, skis, and fishing equipment. More important to the tourist, this is the finest place to rent sports gear—everything from surf-casting rods to sleeping bags.

PARK PRESIDIO SPORTING GOODS, 152 Clement Street, San Francisco. (A large general shop with some rentals.)

Also check the sports departments of the large department stores and discount houses—Emporium, Macy's, G.L.T., et cetera.)

Archery

VIKING SPORTS SPECIALISTS, 1874 Market Street, San Francisco.

THE BOW RACK, 13824 San Pablo Avenue, San Pablo.

SAN FRANCISCO ARCHERY SHOP, 2115 Taraval Street, San Francisco.

All these shops have indoor archery ranges to test your bows before you buy.

Bikes

The bicycle center of San Francisco is on Stanyan Street near Golden Gate Park. There are four bike shops within walking distance of each other that not only sell and repair bikes but rent them as well. If they don't have what you're looking for, they'll tell you where to find it.

Camping

There are several fine retail outlets here which are seen most places only in catalogues. Of course, all general sporting-goods stores sell some of this equipment, but these specialize in stuff directed to the backpacker and camper out.

THE SMILIE CO., 575 Howard Street, San Francisco.

EDDIE BAUER, INC., 120 Kearny Street, San Francisco.

STREETER & QUARLES WEST, 271 Sutter Street, San Francisco.

GeM SALES CO. 1667 Mornet Street, San Francisco.

SIERRA SKI & DIVE, 2123 Junipero Serra Drive, Daly City.

Fencing
AMERICAN FENCERS' SUPPLY CO., 2116 Fillmore Street, San Francisco.

Mountain Climbing
Both these shops can supply you with crampons and pitons.

THE MOUNTAIN SHOP, 228 Grant Avenue, San Francisco.

WEST PORTAL SPORTS, 301 West Portal Avenue, San Francisco.

Team Sports
Your home-town team might want you to price team equipment while you're visiting the big city.

OLYMPIC SPORTING GOODS, 2241 Market Street, San Francisco, can give you a price on anything from basketball uniforms to a gross of handball balls, to a pole-vault pole.

Skin Diving
For skin-diving equipment and/or training, try the following:

BAMBOO REEF ENTERPRISES, 584 Fourth Street, San Francisco; 1111 University Avenue, Berkeley.

SIERRA SKI & DIVE, 2123 Junipero Serra Drive, Daly City.

ED BROWLEY SKIN DIVING SCHOOL, 314 South Bayshore Boulevard, San Mateo.

CALIFORNIA DIVER'S SUPPLY, 630 Octavia Street, San Francisco.

AQUA GEAR SCHOOL OF DIVING, 1254 Ninth Avenue, San Francisco.

And That Ends Sports

Stamps

As with automotive stuff, I don't know a thing about stamps and hesitate to direct you to the best shops. You'll have to explore through the yellow pages of the phone book and make your own discoveries.

Toys

Now there are toy stores and there are toy stores. F. A. O. Schwarz, at 180 Post Street right down from Union Square, is a store every parent with visiting child must see. It's a rich man's store, and so you see only the finest. It's a store kids dream in. You see the exact crenelated castle (selling for $200) that you always wanted; the steam engine that pulls belts of the factory in miniature (going for $245); and the gas-motored dune buggy for kids—that every kid eats his heart out for, and every adult imagines himself at the wheel of—when he was ten and longed for just such a motor—that sells for $695. The good thing about this toy store is that all the toys are there to play with. They were so open that parents parked their kids there and went shopping downtown for a few hours. The kids, of course, abused the display toys, so now it's a rule that if there's a kid in the store there has to be an adult.

THE EMPORIUM (downtown store) has one of the best toy departments of all the downtown stores, but check the others listed in the Handicraft section of this book. Other good stores are:

Toys R'Us, Serramonte Shopping Center off Route 280, Daly City.

JEFFERY'S TOYS, Ghirardelli Square, San Francisco.

KING NORMAN'S KINGDOM OF TOYS, 645 Clement Street, San Francisco.

ARTHUR'S TOY TOWN, 220 Primrose Road, Burlingame.

Foreign Shops and Restaurants

San Francisco and the Bay area are very cosmopolitan—a gathering place for people from all over the world. Kids are fascinated by other cultures and here is a good place to let them shop for foreign souvenirs and eat in foreign restaurants. The list is just a sampling. Because I've tried to cover as wide a range as possible, it's not as deep as it could be—in fact, this subject could be another book in itself.

The best place for a wide range of foreign publications, newspapers, and magazines is HAROLD'S, 405 Geary Street (near Mason), San Francisco. THE EUROPEAN BOOKSTORE, 925 Larkin Street, San Francisco, has a large selection of French, German, and Spanish books, records, and maps. To organize this section, the shops are grouped by continent, then country. Restaurants will follow the shops and designated by (R).

Europe
  English
  EDINBURGH CASTLE, 950 Geary Street. (English and Scottish), San Francisco.
  (R) THE OLD CHELSEA, Fish and chips (oldest and best) 932 Larkin Street, San Francisco.
  Irish
  HOUSE OF IRELAND, 238 O'Farrell Street, San Francisco.
  KILKENNY SHOP, 900 North Point (Ghirardelli Square), San Francisco.
  IRISH CENTER OF SAN FRANCISCO, 2123 Market Street, San Francisco,
  IRISH IMPORTS, 3157 Geary Boulevard, San Francisco.

German

GERMAN SPECIALTIES, 1581 Church Street, San Francisco.

(R) HANS SPECKMAN'S, 1550 Church Street, San Francisco.

(R) RATHSKELLER RESTAURANT, 600 Turk Street, San Francisco.

French

ODETTE ETCHEVERRY FRENCH GIFT SHOP, 1325 Twenty-third Avenue, San Francisco.

TRICOLOR FRENCH RESTAURANT, 4233 Geary Boulevard, San Francisco.

Dutch

BEST OF HOLLAND, Ghirardelli Square, San Francisco.

Scandinavian

CHRISTIAN OF COPENHAGAN, 225 Post Street, San Francisco.

MORNESTAM'S SCANDINAVIAN GIFTS, Ghirardelli Square, San Francisco.

STOCKHOLMIA, 450 Columbus Avenue, San Francisco.

(R) NORSE COVE, 434 Castro Street, San Francisco.

(R) SCANDINAVIAN DELICATESSEN, 2251 Market Street, San Francisco.

(R) LITTLE SWEDEN, 572 O'Farrell Street, San Francisco.

Italian Shops and Restaurants

In North Beach, you'll find many shops with Italian books, records, and craft imports. Many Italian restaurants will be found in the restaurant section of this book.

Greek

HELLENIC-AMERICAN GIFT SHOP, 2365 Mission Street, San Francisco.

GREEK IMPORTS, 132 Eddy Street, San Francisco.

KYRIAKOS OF HYDRA, Ghirardelli Square, San Francisco.

HELLAS IMPORTED FOODS AND CRAFTS (Greek, Syrian, Armenian) 2308 Market Street, San Francisco.

(R) MINERVA CAFÉ, 136 Eddy Street, San Francisco.

Russian

AMERICAN-RUSSIAN INSTITUTE, 90 McAllister Street, San Francisco.

ZNANIE BOOKSTORE, 5237 Geary Boulevard, San Francisco.

(R) BORIS & MARY'S, 301 Balboa Street, San Francisco.

Africa

AFRICAN HUT, 1815 Laguna, Street, San Francisco.

AFRICAN SAFARI, 1221 Divisidero Street, San Francisco.

(No African restaurants that I know of.)

Middle And Near East

Arab (generally)

PERSIAN BAZAAR, 347 Grant Avenue, San Francisco.

SAMIRAMIS IMPORTS, 2998 Mission Street, San Francisco.

RABAT NORTH AFRICAN IMPORTS, 746 Diamond Street, San Francisco.

(R) OMAR KHAYAMS, 196 O'Farrell Street, San Francisco.

Israeli

LIEBER'S HEBREW-ENGLISH BOOK AND GIFT SHOP, 5445 Geary Boulevard, San Francisco.

ISRAEL IMPORTS, 5542 Geary Boulevard, San Francisco.

THE BOOK SHOOK, 2440 Noriega Street, San Francisco.

(R) DAVID'S, 474 Geary Street, San Francisco

(R) SOLOMAN'S KOSHER STYLE, 424 Geary Street, San Francisco.

India

INDIAN BAZAAR IMPORTS, 697 Sutter Street, San Francisco.

INDIA CARGO INTERNATIONAL, 1263 Mission Street, San Francisco.

INDIAN IMPORTS, INC., 121 O'Farrell Street, San Francisco.

INDIAN GIFTS AND FOODS, 643 Post Street, San Francisco.

(R) INDIA HOUSE RESTAURANT, 350 Jackson Street, San Francisco.

Far East

China

Chinatown is the main locus of Chinese shops and restaurants. Although the shops in Chinatown now sell goods from mainland China, two stores outside Chinatown specialize in mainland Chinese things.

THE CULTURAL REVOLUTION, 2102 Union Street San Francisco.

CHINA BOOKS, 2929 Twenty-fourth Street, San Francisco.

Japan

Japantown is the place to go for all kinds of Japanese things. See the Restaurants section for some good Japanese restaurants outside the area.

Philippines

One of the most interesting shops in town is KAPIT-BHAY, 1201 Geneva Avenue, near Naples Street, San Francisco. This is a Philippine, Oriental, Hawaiian supermarket with the most incredible line of exotic foods I've ever seen. Here you can buy canned coconut milk, poi, and fresh-frozen banana leaves and cassava. The frozen-fish department includes flat-headed goby, bungus, and sap-sap (these fish look as though they were freshly taken from a coral reef and should be swimming in an aquarium somewhere). There are canned exotic fruits of the South Seas—

tamarind, guava, papaya, jack fruit, and we musn't forget banana blossoms. There are nine kinds of noodle, as well as sago palm starch. Some things for sale make you wonder. Salted watermelon seeds are packaged for sale, for example, and you wonder why we just spit them out instead of roasting and salting them as we do pumpkin and sunflower seeds? The greatest thing about this store is that they sell these exotic things with no show and no fanfare; they sell imported banana ice cream from Manila as casually as the grocery up the street sells pork and beans. This shop gives kids a closer look at the cultures of the South Pacific than a whole block of crafts shops would.

North and South America

North American Indian

For those interested in American Indian things, the best place to see fine examples is the De Young Museum, San Francisco, or the Lowic Museum at the University of California at Berkeley. For those kids who are itching to buy their own authentic Indian artifact or craft, I've listed a few stores where you can find them. Be warned, these places are not cheap.

ARCHIVES, 2196 Union Street, San Francisco.

BAZAAR CADA DIA, 2801 Leavenworth—402 Sutter Street, San Francisco.

WEST OF THE MOON, 3464 Sacramento Street, San Francisco.

DAVIDSON INDIAN HANDICRAFT, 1829 Union Street, San Francisco.

Central and South America

Like Chinatown, Japantown, and North Beach, the part of the Mission District around Twenty-fourth Street is also a cultural center. Here the common bond is not culture, race, or nationality, but the Spanish language. When people think of the Spanish language, the first thing that comes to mind is Mexico. Much of the American Southwest and Far West was once Mexican; Mexico is our nearest neighbor to the south.

It's often forgotten that right down the coast are Nicaragua, El Salvador, Costa Rica, Guatamala, Colombia, Bolivia, Chile, and Peru. There are large numbers of folks from all these different cultures living in San Francisco today. Their common bond is the Spanish language, but each is as distinct as the Englishman is from the Irishman (something seen every Sunday at the Balboa Soccer Stadium, where each nationality fields its own team). There are Peruvian, Nicaraguan, Guatamalan, Argentinian, Costa Rican, and many regional Mexican restaurants in this area. The shops, grocery stores, crafts shops of all kinds can be found on Mission Street from about Twentieth Street to Army and along Twenty-fourth Street to Potrero. This is a relatively new cultural center in San Francisco and is slowly congealing into a major tourist center of "Spanish"-Americans. The grocery stores are interesting, stocking as they do yucca root and plantain as staples. It's a wonderful discovery area for the whole family.

SANCHEZ SPANISH BOOK AND MUSIC STORE, 2130 Mission Street.

LIBRERIA MEXICO, 2631 Mission Street.

These stores are long established and can give you good information.

24

Restaurants

The second biggest daily problem of a touring family (and a continuing one for Bay area families) is where to feed the kids. This doesn't pose much of a problem in smaller towns where there only two restaurants to choose between. In a city like San Francisco, though, world famous for fine food, it's difficult to know where to go—especially if you have children with you. Fortunately, the restaurants serving our two most famous cuisines, Chinese and Italian, follow almost universally a general pattern beloved by San Franciscans and tourists alike—that is, good food, lots of it, and bring the kids. In both Chinatown and North Beach, you and your family can walk into any restaurant you see (whether mentioned in this book or not) and are almost guaranteed to enjoy the food. Many of the restaurants serve family style; most have children's plates and, in the Chinese restaurants, it's almost universally true that if you order a family dinner for three, there's food enough for at least four, and an extra place setting can be ordered at a nominal charge. Most of the restaurants listed here are in the moderate-to-reasonable range, but I will include a few elegant places (that like children) for that extra-special touch to your visit to San Francisco. I cannot quote prices because it is impossible these days, as you well know. I will list only places that have been here for a million years and will be here when you visit. Some restaurants require reservations and some are closed on Mondays or Tuesdays. It's best to call before you go. All, though, are special, good places you'll remember.

Hot Dogs and Hamburgers

If you're interested in lunch or a light supper where you're going to have hot dogs or hamburgers anyway, you might as well go to good places instead of the instant-heartburn franchise joints. These places are very fine.

THE HIPPO, 2025 Van Ness Avenue, San Francisco. This is a hamburger palace. It sells maybe a million different kinds of hamburgers, including Giraffeburgers, Gorillaburgers, Polynesianburgers and Cannibalburgers. Reasonable, fun, and good.

BILL'S PLACE, 2315 Clement Street, San Francisco. Have your hamburger in an outdoor garden.

THE NOBLE FRANKFURTER, 529 Powell and 3159 Fillmore Street, San Francisco.

These places simply serve the best hot dogs in town.

Something Very Special for Kids

MARIN PIZZA PUB, 526 third Street, San Rafael.

In how many places in the country featuring live music, could you request a number from the musician that would include fire sirens, train whistles, and horses' hoofs—and have your request played! You can at the pizza pub. Smack in the middle of this pizza parlor is the keyboard of a huge old theater organ that has enough sound effects to re-create the Creation. Some of the instruments, like snare drums, horses hoofs, and castanets are in the main room, but the ranks upon ranks of pipes for the organ (from piccolo to ships' whistles) are in two large, glassed rooms in the rear of the place, where you can watch them in operation. This pizza parlor is always full of kids and I can't exactly describe the feeling of glee that overcomes you when the organist swings into "The Stars and Stripes Forever" with cymbals crashing, the revolving mirrored ball in the ceiling sweeping the room with points of light, the bubble machines on the walls making the room look like the inside of a glass of champagne, the floor vibrating from the big organ booming all stops out, the kids going crazy. It's deafening and delightful, and the pizza isn't bad either. Call for performance times.

Family Style, Buffet, Smorgasbord

No one ever left hungry from these good places.

GARDEN COURT, Sheraton Palace Hotel, San Francisco. This is an elegant place that serves a beautiful buffet. Not too outrageously expensive.

GOLD SPIKE, 527 Columbus Avenue, San Francisco. (Family-style Italian.)

LITTLE SWEDEN, 572 O'Farrell Street, San Francisco (Smorgasbord.)

UNIVERSAL CAFÉ, 826 Washington Street, San Francisco. (Chinese.)

KUO WAH, 950 Grant Avenue, San Francisco. (Chinese.)

GOLDEN DRAGON, 816 Washington Street, San Francisco. (Chinese.)

JOE JUNG'S, 881 Clay Street, San Francisco. (Chinese.)

MINGEI YA, 2033 Union Street, San Francisco. (Japanese country inn style.)

Z's BOUNTIFUL BUFFET, Geary & Arguello Boulevards, San Francisco. (American buffet.)

RISTORANTE ITALIANO, 622 Green Street, San Francisco. (Family-style Italian.)

GREEN VALLEY CAFÉ, 510 Green Street, San Francisco. (Family-style Italian.)

General

CAESAR'S, Bay and Powell Streets, San Francisco. (Italian.)

CHUCK WAGON, 215 West Portal Avenue, San Francisco. (American.)

FIO D' ITALIA, 621 Union Street, San Francisco.

FLEUR DE FRANCE, 3148 Geary Boulevard, San Francisco.

GRISON'S STEAK & CHOP HOUSE, 2100 Van Ness Avenue, San Francisco.

LUCHINA RUSSIAN RESTAURANT, 1829 Clement Street, San Francisco.

MINERVA CAFÉ, 136 Eddy Street, San Francisco. (Greek.)

SCHROEDER'S CAFÉ, 240 Front Street, San Francisco. (German.)

TORTOLA, 1237 Polk Street, San Francisco. (Mexican.)

LITTLE FIESTA, 2801 Geary Street, San Francisco. (Mexican.)

VICTORIA STATION, 50 Broadway, San Francisco.

LA PIÑATA, 1851 Union Street, San Francisco. (Mexican.)

Seafood

Being near the ocean, you might want to try our good seafood restaurants.

A. SABELLA'S, Fisherman's Wharf, San Francisco.

BERNSTEIN'S FISH GROTTO, 123 Powell Street, San Francisco.

CASTIGNOLA, 286 Jefferson Street, Fisherman's Wharf, San Francisco.

EXPOSITION FISH GROTTO, Fisherman's Wharf, San Francisco.

FISHERMAN'S GROTTO No. 9, Fisherman's Wharf, San Francisco.

POMPEI'S GROTTO, 340 Jefferson Street, Fisherman's Wharf, San Francisco.

SPENCER'S FISH GROTTO, 1919 Fourth Street, Berkeley.

SABELLA'S, 555 Redwood Highway, Mill Valley. (Off Highway 101.)

Index

IN THE CITY
THAT BLOWS YOUR MIND

HERE AT LAST IS THE GUIDE
THAT WILL BLOW YOUR MIND

Know the city as you have never known it before, whether
you explore it on foot, by San Francisco's celebrated transportation, or as an armchair tourist.

Revel in a book you will read and re-read, before your arrival, during your stay, and after your departure, for information and for sheer enjoyment.

In a city so old that every nook and cranny holds a colorful
story—and so young that the shadows of the founding
fathers still fall on its cosmopolitan streets—you want to get
beyond the standard guide to a splendor that is totally
unique. AN OPINIONATED GUIDE TO SAN FRAN-
CISCO gets you there, and leaves you breathless.

Revised 1974 Edition

AN OPINIONATED GUIDE
TO SAN FRANCISCO
by Franz T. Hansell

No visit is complete without it

$1.95

available at your local bookstore